Leena

with love

Steve E !

RELATIONSHIPS IN RECOVERY

RELATIONSHIPS IN RECOVERY

*A Guide to Building Safe and
Sustainable Partnerships in Sobriety*

My Bridge to Normal Living Series

Steve E

Relationships in Recovery
ISBN-13: 9798556399853
November 2020 First Edition

The author is not affiliated with Alcoholics Anonymous or any other
twelve step recovery programme.

LOVE AND PEACE

We think of conflicts and injustices around the world as the great destroyers of peace. But for many of us, peace is given or denied by the personal relationships we have.

Addiction is a sad failing of the human condition, but there is a way-out for a few lucky ones. Yet so many who find sobriety are still denied love because of problems with personal relationships.

Love and peace – I hope I can help you find these things.

TABLE OF CONTENTS

Chapter One – Setting the Scene

Through the end of my drinking days and into early recovery, part of my journey was the collapse of a marriage and divorce. After that, I was single for a few years, dated a few times, then had one five-year relationship that ultimately did not work. Now, after fifteen years of sobriety, I'm finally in a marriage that's just amazing. But that didn't happen by luck, or my higher-power alone.

In the early years of my recovery, it became clear to me that there was not enough discussion, guidance or literature in the area of personal relationships. So I started to work on some ideas myself. Relationships are very difficult for all humans it seems. If we look at our family, friends and work colleagues, we see relationship problems and unhappiness everywhere. For us alcoholics, we soon discover that our early lives and drinking days were useless for learning anything other than how to be selfish and get drunk. Add to that the greedy and sexist society that we live in and you can see that we alcoholics haven't got much of a chance of understanding personal relationships at all.

I also realised that for many alcoholics, problems with relationships, sex or loneliness, matters so often swept under the AA carpet, are driving them back to a drink. In the fellowship, we work so hard in almost every other area to support people's development and reduce their unmanageability, but when it comes to relationships I don't think we do anything like enough.

Who This Book is For

I'm aiming this book at those who are well into a twelve step recovery program and want to get better at the business of relationships.

I'm in AA, so my thinking is very much along the lines of AA, but I understand that other twelve step programs are pretty similar so I think my book would apply to those groups too. This book might also be of some use if you are not in recovery, although knowledge of twelve step processes is important to properly understand some of the chapters.

And maybe those who are still drinking might see this book – and like seeing the Big Book for the first time, it might give hope that our lives can be better in the future.

I'm writing at a similar depth to the AA book 'The Twelve Steps and Twelve Traditions' (Twelve and Twelve). I feel I should always be fairly specific, in a similar way to how the Twelve and Twelve deals with the steps in more detail when you compare it to the Big Book. For me, the issue with softer suggestions is that I would often not do them. And this is clearly identified in step five in the Twelve and Twelve, where it says that left to our own devices we won't see the truth. For example, most people start off by thinking that we do our inventory on our own, write the list and look at it, then finally share it with someone else, and God (with a couple of coffees and a quick prayer). The Twelve and Twelve says if we work this simplistically, we will remain self-deceiving.

Put it another way. Try on your own to write the instructions to refurbish a rocket engine. Rocket engines are hugely stressed and almost burned to a crisp after a launch (a bit like us), so to write a rocket engine maintenance plan without extensive rocket engine knowledge would be nuts. We simply have to learn from, and work with, other people in order to get it right. In our case, that's a sponsor, our fellowship friends and if we're in a relationship, a partner too.

In my early recovery, my sponsor would repeatedly tell me about ego reduction, and how I could become teachable. This would often result in him actually telling me to do, or not to do something – that is, I should do something I didn't want to do, or not to do something I wanted to do. When I became teachable, and did what he said, I experienced the benefit of better decisions. So, if specific things could help my recovery, perhaps specifics could also improve my chances of a good relationship.

Also, in some ways this book is like a very long share from me to you – from recovery buddy to recovery buddy. And as you would in the rooms, please take what you like and leave the rest. Perhaps after reading some of it you can talk about these things with your partner, sponsor and friends. You can use this work to explore your own ideas about relationships in recovery because really, if you properly apply the twelve steps to this issue, I think you'll come up with the same answers as I did anyway. I also presume that readers would understand the risk of big egos and 'self will run riot', the advantage of some form of higher power in our lives, and the need for a vital spiritual experience or psychic change great enough to bring about recovery.

I have developed ideas about how we behave in quite primeval ways in relationships and how men and women are different. I have expanded on how the steps might be used to jointly build a relationship that works more effectively with both our alcoholic behaviours and human instincts. I have looked at the issue of dating, the management of practical matters, and the structures required for a good long-term relationship.

Then I think it comes down to the reader's desire to have a real good think about relationships. Everything that happens to us, from early childhood right through into sobriety, plus our past relationship experiences, all have a huge affect on our relationship prospects now.

Important Concepts

There are two important concepts that I use throughout the book that require some early definition.

One – In Love and the In-love Instinct:

I realised that I couldn't just use the word love on its own. We soon learn in the Fellowship that the word love can mean many different types of love – God's love, love of ones fellows, parental love and so-on. So I will use 'in-love' to mean that focussed, romantic love between a couple (of any sexual orientation). And I have deliberately used 'in' to identify that this emotion is much more specific in its character because we are either usually strongly 'in' it with someone, or we are definitely not. It's a very rapid emotion sometimes and as teenage girlfriends might tease each other "you're so in love with him ha ha." The signs and symptoms are much more obvious and distinctly different from all other types of love.

So through the book I develop the idea that in-love is a separate instinct from the security, social and sex instincts. I found that I could not explain big parts of the problems and behaviours around relationships without putting the drivers into the category of a separate instinct. And not the sex instinct, they seem to be clearly different to me.

Two – The Responsibility Burden:

It says in the big book 'we are responsible.' The responsibility that should exist between partners in a relationship is a very big issue in my view. We learn that we must be honest and good to everyone we meet in life because this is the true output of the good character we need to find in sobriety. But most of all we have a huge responsibility to be good to our partners.

We talk at great length in recovery about the children, parents and old spouses – those we hurt so badly during our drinking days. We discuss how the most fundamental amends we can make to these people is to stop drinking and thus stop filling them with fear. We learn how to put others before ourselves as St Francis did, otherwise we may fall back into our selfish ways again. But we don't talk so much about responsibilities in new personal relationships, at least not to the depth that we should. And there's one very big reason why we have to pay special attention here because not only do we have to protect our partner's general instincts, wellbeing and so-on as we do with everyone else around us, but we are going to create a new and very powerful instinct within that person; their in-love instinct, and it's going to be focussed solely on us. This is a position of huge responsibility.

The God Thing

A close recovery buddy, confidant and advisor of mine strongly suggested I removed any references to God from this book. His reason was it would put some readers off. I couldn't do it.

I believe that if Bill W and the First One Hundred thought God should be central to our recovery programme, written deep into the essence of the Big Book and the Twelve and Twelve, then that's how it should be. I worked hard writing this book, but they worked harder, much harder, to come up with the fundamentals that have saved us all. Sure, as individuals we can pick the higher-power of our choice – the purpose is to ensure we don't try and stay in control. But I can't help thinking our founders were on to something – it works better with God in it.

Right up to the end of my drinking, I believed I was the only entity that knew what was going on. Everyone, every organisation and everything with authority was wrong. You were all idiots – period. So what was going to break that thinking? For me it was a change of outlook on power. I used to think I was empowered. We hear the word empowered all the time in modern society and everyone thinks it's a good thing, but most recovering alcoholics spend half their lives working out that for us it's not. You see, I'm still an idiot and can never risk being empowered. Believing in God helps me remember this. In essence I must use Gods power, not my own – mine doesn't work properly.

My early recovery also included a lot of involvement in modern church. Again, no more intended than having to go to my first AA meetings – pure fear of relapse was the driver. There too (I couldn't always get to AA meetings) I found productive people who were not self-empowered. And in church I found love, kindness and a message – and guess what – in essence it's the same message as in the Big Book. So which ever way we cut it, which ever way we care to debate about the presence of God and the parental line of Jesus, I just don't think it's worth us (as individuals who truly don't know any better) having a strong opinion against it.

Through the book I refer to God in the way that works for me. In detailed ways that directly help specific problems. I try to be clear with the part of my relationship with God that I am using. It might be for example how I have faith that he will protect me if some sudden adverse or dangerous situation should occur. Now this reliance on God, for me, mostly comes from real experience. Events that were really as strange and unexpected to me as they might sound to you. Then as my recovery improved, and my life got better and better, I came to see that the rate and quality of that improvement seemed to depend on how much I asked God for knowledge of his will for me.

And for those that are not sure I would simply say, remember the line about contempt prior to investigation. It might take twenty or thirty years for you to complete that investigation.

One final thing – I know a lot of people who have God in their lives and it always looks to me like they have happier and more rewarding relationships than those who don't.

What About The Women's Point Of View?

Many women helped me write this book. Without a huge input from women, this book would be useless. And whilst there were lots of conversations about the obvious issues of relationships, what was particularly fruitful was analysing the deep differences in the perception and thinking processes of men and women. I listened carefully to the woman's views of men, and the men's views of women – this revealed huge flaws in both our understanding of and actions between the two sexes.

I had many discussions with women about their relationship experiences before and after they found sobriety. I looked for both the objective and emotional reasons why women struggle in this area and I discovered something important – on the surface, men and women appear different in their needs and fears around relationships but deep down, and in real spiritual and wellbeing terms, there is not much difference at all. Our perceptions are masked by so many misunderstandings and our true needs are buried under the fear or resignation that it can't be better.

Some women are fearful and very cautious about men. They have good reason to be. Both men and women behave very badly in life, but men can often be more brutal or unforgiving in their actions, and women can be more oversensitive or retaliatory when scorned. These things need to be looked at in all of us. Many men and women also look at the opposite sex as just that – opposite. And women sometimes more so than men. The classic example is women seem to blame men for their sex instinct but the truth is the genetic code that drives it is the property of the whole human race, not just men.

When I asked women what they want from a relationship now, in recovery (often having been battered and bruised by terrible experiences in the past), they want the love of a kind man who brings responsibility and security. Men, it is clear to me that if you want to step up and do it right and really sweep a girl off her feet, you have to do way better than you ever did before.

Talking to Partners About AA

Discussing AA with a partner who doesn't know much about the fellowship can be incredibly tricky, so it's worth flagging this up early. I always think the best place to start is The Doctor's Opinion in the Big Book, where the doctor's letters describe many aspects of the condition of alcoholism and the AA programme of spiritual recovery – a professional's observation as to it's effectiveness. Starting here means you can avoid going straight in talking about God, how meetings work and so-on.

Usefully for us, the doctor's letters say that whilst many people think stopping drinking is just a matter of exerting one's willpower, his observations did not support this. It may be helpful to say that in the other people of your AA group, you have found a common experience – they all suffer from the inability to stop the craving for alcohol by using their own willpower in isolation, but they found they could with the collective power of the AA group. You can say that listening to their stories about lack of willpower, chaos and fear is enlightening for you, that you can already see you have the same problem. And that they, through AA, have found the solution.

You can also use The Doctor's Opinion to describe AA's answer to what alcoholism is – the obsession of the mind and the allergy of the body – again a question that might often be asked of you in the early days.

And also, related to partners and family issues, I have on many occasions been surprised how unaware many AA folk are of chapters eight and nine in The Big Book. Try it for yourself – ask an AA buddy what the title of these chapters are, and the essence of what they contain. I'll give you evens they won't know. Chapter eight, 'To Wives' and chapter nine 'The family afterwards' provide essential knowledge to us all in recovery, and not just those thinking about making good on romantic relationships. One of the important thing about these chapters, I think, is they show us how the damage caused by the alcoholic in families was identified and treated with such significance right back at the start of AA. Indeed, we know this was the start of Bill's wife Lowis' work in the formation of Al Anon.

In chapter eight of the Big Book, there is a good description of the general state of the alcoholic in a severely stressed relationship, put from the point of view of the suffering wife or husband. It breaks down the condition the alcoholic might be in, into four worsening states. Again, this maybe an important piece of information the alcoholic might want to use to lay some foundations in a recoverable relationship, so check it out.

And chapter nine is essential study material too. It covers a broad range of family issues, with children, finance and so-on. And it explains how the family may take quite some time to change and accept the possibility of improvement through recovery.

Anyway, there's no need for me to describe these chapters any more. I simply raise it here to give you early awareness of them.

Negativity Towards AA

It's a strange world we live in. For example, why are people such opposites in their basic character – some full of loving and giving and some full of hatred and cynicism. I believe the more good you try to do, in your thinking and actions, the happier you'll be. I also believe it's vital to learn from other people, and that contempt prior to investigation is a sad problem for so many.

If you have read reviews on Amazon about recovery books you will see lots of divided opinion. People in AA mostly love this fellowship but there are others who call AA a cult and say it's all about religious indoctrination, that its principles are too negative (supposedly we have all lost our willpower) and that to suggest surrender is just a way to make people compliant. Compliant to what, I would ask? The opposition, in essence, say that we should just say no (to addiction), and snap ourselves out of it. Well to that I say fine, if you can do it. But of course I couldn't. I needed to surrender – in the end that turns out to be the much wiser thing to do for me.

There's a lot written about the low success rate of AA, that short-term intervention by medical experts is more successful. Well maybe it's more successful at stopping people picking up a drink, for a while. But I honestly can't see how that would have brought me the great benefit that AA has given me – my bridge to normal living. Recovery, AA style, is a life long programme because we need to learn how to live – a fundamental that we totally missed when we were drinking. We have to deal with new problems in our lives, as they arise, and I haven't heard of anyone producing a drug yet that stops life's problems from occurring (we stupidly thought booze could do that). Without AA, I for one would always fail in life, then go back to a drink.

Now, when we come on to the topic of relationships and AA, we should discuss what might be described as sexual predators in the rooms. Often known in the Fellowship as thirteen stepping. It does go on, and I think to a certain extent it's understandable (not acceptable). When people first come to AA they are very vulnerable, particularly when they discover the early joys of recovery (the pink fluffy cloud) and a strong supportive figure can easily take advantage of that. But remember two things, firstly the vulnerable newcomer possibly would have had a similarly inappropriate liaison just a few weeks ago down the pub, and secondly the 13 stepper, whilst seeming strong in their recovery has, like most of us, failed to learn anything about relationships. So please be careful with your criticism against either party. Heck, it's because we don't talk about these things enough that I'm writing this book. If anything, literally anything, is wrong with either an individual or people collectively in the rooms, it's only because we are not doing enough work about the problem. Some people have fights in the rooms, others flirt. We have to face these things and deal with them responsibly.

And many people in the fellowship are lonely on a personal level. Remember we're aiming at in-balance instincts not zero instincts, so surely it can be a thing of joy all around if people in recovery start a good relationship. If you take a look at what's happened, you have a bunch of people who were all self-centred, selfish individuals living in the isolation of booze and unmanageability, who have suddenly sprung into a world of companionship and love.

Books, Doctors and Counsellors

Most doctors, counsellors and other support professionals never experience the problems we go through. Of course, as people they must have their fair share of problems, but your doctor is probably not a recovering alcoholic. However, even if he was, the professional boundary that doctors use means they can never share their personal experiences with you. So the process never feels two-way, or close, or anything like the shared realisation that you're both in the same boat. You're never going to be in that fellowship situation with your doctor or counsellor.

Therefore your doctor's advice is likely coming from a powerpoint lecture she once saw, or your counsellor will be trying to categorise you into one of the problem groups he wrote about for his degree thesis. Councillors run a session for a fixed hour, then try to tell us what to do, or much worse, we walk out of a doctor's appointment with a prescription for anti-depressants. So for you and me, these things can never really do it. When you come into the fellowship, it's a mutual process. And with my research for this book I've found that learning about relationships is a mutual process also. I think after you've experienced the results from your AA meetings and the steps, you will feel a book on relationships based on a doctor's scientific analysis (from case studies of other people) doesn't carry much weight at all.

I looked at some of the relationship books written by doctors and there were massive issues with those for me. First, there really was no reference to any personal experience. Second, they're full of jargon, cross references and footnotes, all in a very confusing layout. And finally there is the requirement for the publication to be approved by 'peer review' – a formal academic process that all scientists put their writing through before it gets published. The problem is, this process creates a fear that the establishment will see them as stepping out of line if they write anything new, yet they want to publish something for their CV and own financial gain. And when it comes to our type of recovery and spiritual wellbeing, well for most doctors and scientists, our solution, our way of thinking, is just too left-field for them.

I've had quite a few other people helping me with this book, so that's sort of a peer review I suppose. But the difference is we're doing it for other people, not ourselves. Ah, that's not quite true, as with sponsoring, our own recoveries and relationships have improved immensely because we've been doing this work. But also, I don't mind at all if people don't like what I've written. I have no career (just a moderate ego) dependent on it.

And here's another flaw in the system. Didn't we learn early on that drunks only ever get understanding from, and open up to, other drunks. We almost never tell doctors or councillors the truth. Professionals study others, like rats in a lab, but if we alcoholics rarely tell doctor's the truth, then those people are working from incorrect data.

Communication

Communication comes up all the way through the book. But I raise the topic here to flag that it's such an important issue to consider right from the start. With me for example, it affects how I'm writing these words, and for you, how you are reading them. Communication is affected greatly by our backgrounds, attitudes and perceptions, I've found, and the combination of these factors can unwittingly create significant problems with our understanding of each other.

Here's one example from my own past. And I'm going to give quite a bit of detail here to show how the mechanisms of communication style can be quite complex. I was in the British Royal Air Force for 22 years and trained as an engineer officer. In early training, one of the many things you're taught is how you should make quick decisions, stick to those decisions and then implement them. In essence, how to carry through the things you have decided upon. You learn how to pass down your orders to your subordinates who may not like or agree with what you've decided to do. But if you give in to their questioning or differences of opinion, you lose track of your task, you're not really in command, and your team is now making decisions by committee. So your instructors hammer into you that you must make your plan quickly, then stick to it – you might ask for input during your early planning, but then no more. So in the past, my style of communication became characterised by this 'make a quick decision and stick to it at all costs' mentality that meant I might say something and then later not want to say any more on the matter. Down the line of course, this proved very tricky for relationships and it was surprisingly hard to shift the habit, or even be aware of it.

Your communication style and effectiveness is something you can analyse by the inventory process. In our inventories we look at resentments, fears and so-on, and that is for certain the right place to start, but relationships are a whole extra dimension of normal living and doing an inventory on our communication style can be incredibly useful.

Some Things about Me

I think I'm quite an optimist. I'm enthusiastic for things that are important. I'll say yes to almost anything now – good things, spiritual things. And I try and follow things through.

Many years ago I was criticised in a work appraisal (in my drinking days) for starting tasks with good ideas and great enthusiasm, but then not completing the work well. I was hurt because it was true, and I've always been much more determined to complete things since that report. My boss at the time was one of those people who made a lasting impact on my work attitudes. One thing he used to say was "play the long game, Steve", a cricket expression I believe. He meant, apply careful analysis with lots of patience and keep your sights fixed on your goal, no matter how long it takes – a vital tip for writing books and success in relationships of course. My failings at that time had been caused by my desire to impress at the start, then laziness to complete the work. I hope I'm not like that now.

I'm reasonably well educated in engineering, management and business but don't have any qualifications in medicine, psychology or the like. All of this book is derived from my own life experiences, and the experiences of my wife, Kathryn, quite a few family and friends, and a lot of recovery buddies. Every now and then through the book, I describe some of my and Kathryn's experiences in detail. These honest anecdotes are about our problems, the mistakes we have made and how they have subsequently come to help us make progress. And I've already made a few jokes about my ego – only because if I didn't still have a bit of an over-inflated ego, I might never have written this book.

For context here are some specifics about Kathryn, and I. I have been sober since December 2005 and Kathryn has been sober since March 2014. I met Kathryn in AA in October 2014 and we were married in June 2018.

Finally, I'm not particularly good at written English. I've done a lot of writing in my life, and even done some long courses on written english (management style). But I struggled on those courses with grammar. I'm an engineer by trade, so writing doesn't come that easy to me.

Chapter Two – Wants, Needs, Risks and Situations

In this chapter I set out a list of things that at first seem rather disconnected, but need to be looked at together in order to see just how big the footprint is with relationship issues for us. I have found that other publications start at the point of the problem; you know – "my wife and I aren't speaking, what should we do?" Which is answered by; "you have to tell her how you are feeling". Good grief, if only it was that easy.

Anyway, a broad framework is where we need to start I think, and we need to be grounded in the reality of ourselves and our situations in life. I've heard many people talk honestly about their recoveries, their defects of character, doing the steps, service and so-on, then when it comes to relationship issues, all logic goes out the window.

Correctly Identifying Wants and Needs

The first thing we should do is establish the difference between wants and needs. I will be using those words in this book quite specifically as follows:

- Need – an action or outcome that if not satisfied will have a significant negative impact on our recovery or wellbeing.

- Want – an action or outcome that may have either a moderate positive or moderate negative impact on our recovery or wellbeing.

You could assume that you can live by just needs alone, but that's not much fun. Sensible and realistic wants are very important, they form our bridge to normal living when we get down to the detail. But remember how disastrous our wants were in our drinking days? We always wanted the wrong things – a fundamental fault of the alcoholic and a trap we can easily fall into in sobriety, particularly when the opportunity for a new relationship comes along. So we need balance and we don't need too many wants, if that makes sense, but neither can we live in a vacuum. We do need some things in our life that we want – as long as we understand, and are able to manage, the consequences.

Looking at things in this way, perhaps the first important need should be reason. We need some ability to reason – to sort, with correct logic, the good from the bad. Not being able to reason leads us straight into our unhealthy wants. And good reasoning is largely an output of good honesty. So the simple process is honesty > good reasoning > good actions. You could put this a different way; it's good decision making.

In early recovery we're very bad at reasoning and making decisions. This is something we have to work on a lot as we progress through the steps. As we look back we can see how alcoholism severely degraded our reasoning ability for sure, but also we can see how relationships did this too. This is why our recoveries and our relationships have to be quite closely connected in the way we work them in my view. For example if we learn how to apply much better honesty to our drinking problem, and quickly see the positive results that brings, we should benefit in the same way from applying honesty in the area of relationships.

So how do we correctly identify wants and needs? Below I give examples of what I think are the key needs and wants in respect to relationships. But you should do your own list – this would be a great thing to share with your sponsor and partner.

We Need Sobriety

I don't know about you, but what I need more than anything is sobriety. My sobriety is more important than any relationship. But look, that statement sounds so obvious, surely no one would risk their sobriety by having a bad relationship? But we often do risk it. I think a relationship can be the second most risky thing to your sobriety after booze – and it's easy to see why. The complex emotional situations within a relationship are some of the hardest emotions to be honest about. And a relationship is driven in some part by our most basic instincts. In a relationship we are both dependent on, and responsible to, another person at great depth.

If your first need is sobriety, then your second need is your programme of recovery. But in a relationship it's all too easy to let the correct priorities get pushed out. I've seen it happen with other people quite a few times and the result is always the same – a big mess.

Like alcohol, romantic conquest and romantic attention are hugely powerful forces. The sex drive and perceived need for romance can turn people quite mad, literally – if they don't have a strong enough defence. Indeed, when a relationship starts, you're going to have to work harder on your recovery than at just about any other time. And also remember that time itself is a factor here – what starts out as a sweet and easy relationship can soon build to be a significant complexity in your life, with lots of drama and turmoil. I'll discuss complexity more later.

Of course, on paper this seems pretty obvious but you must keep the priorities the right way up. And vitally, make sure that you and your partner both believe completely this is how it has to be. Anything the two of you may want, or plan for, will be lost if one or both of you undermine the need for effective recovery.

We Need Spiritual Wellbeing in a Relationship

We often define ourselves as physical, mental and spiritual beings. And it's the spiritual aspect that often causes confusion. We're not sure if spiritual is a religious term that means people have to go to church, or is someone only spiritual when they have found God? Or on the other hand is it a concept about peace of mind, or appreciating the very simple things in life like a country walk?

Of course, it talks in step twelve about having had a spiritual awakening as a result of the steps – we might say it's the personality change that enables us to do the will of our higher power. But when we gain more experience we realise that the step-twelve spiritual awakening is like week-one training when we start a new job – you do the basic courses and know, in theory, how to do the job, but that's nowhere near to being fully up-to-speed. That's going to take years to achieve. We do all the earlier steps to learn how to let go of our self will, clean shop and make amends. And after just some of that, we get a glimpse of spirituality – a place where we feel content that we are doing God's will, rather than resenting it. It's funny how that word resentment links to spiritual wellbeing – just think about it; if you don't resent doing something, you don't feel uncomfortable about it. That lack of discomfort is a form of spiritual wellbeing.

But now we have to consider how that wellbeing is maintained in a relationship. One of the biggest things here is that the enemy of spiritual wellbeing is complexity and unmanageability, and a relationship always adds to the management burden. How many times have you started a relationship and said to yourself "well, this makes things easier", then later it always seems to get a lot more complicated? In essence, relationships directly risk our spiritual wellbeing.

And it's no good striving for a spiritual awakening from the insanity of alcoholism, and spiritual wellbeing from your journey through the steps, without all the other major factors in your life being spiritually correct also. If a relationship is spiritually sick, it's not going to work, just like your recovery wouldn't. I don't mean a relationship has to be that you are both in recovery, or has some other structured spiritual program such as religion. No, I mean it must not be spiritually bankrupt. It must be honest and fulfilling, make you both feel safe and secure, and be enjoyable. And don't forget that other things in your life need to be spiritually stable as well if they're not going to become a problem for you and your relationship. Jobs and kids are a couple of prime examples. Spiritual wellbeing across the board is what we need.

We Need Some Planning

At the end of our drinking days we soon see that we don't really have any practical plan for our lives. We've likely wrecked whatever future we thought we would have. In recovery we learn that we should not try and control; all those selfish wants have to stop and we learn how to let go and hand over. But eventually we are going to have to follow some sort of gentle plan.

In early sobriety we usually have a strange period of 'suspended animation'. Things sort of stop for a while. Perhaps we're in an institution that is looking after us, perhaps we're back in our parents home, or maybe we are living with our partner and children, but the situation is very strained because of the damage our drinking has caused. After a while, with the guidance of our fellows and sponsor, we should start some gentle reconstruction of our practical situation. This must be done within the bounds of our recovery, so manageable things that are practical, simple and affordable (financially) such as getting new accommodation, a car and a job. In the early days though, this should not include any change to your relationship situation if that can be avoided. If you are in a relationship that is on shaky ground don't rush to change anything, just start making practical amends the best you can.

Over a longer period though, you need to consider a simple life plan. And you can do this with your sponsor. Remember, we can still be very childish or dramatic in early sobriety – planning grandiose living or maudlin isolation is not on the path of humility, and that's why we often need guidance.

And then, some time later, when our thoughts turn to relationships, a lot more planning will be required. Just be aware of this for now, it will come up in more detail later in the book.

We Want Companionship

Maybe companionship is like fellowship. When we first enter the rooms of AA, we're numb, drained and isolated. But then, perhaps for the first time, we find we can relate to other people with a common experience. And when we are warmed by the care and love that is directed towards us by other members, followed by the joy of helping others, we start to feel the rewards of fellowship.

During our drinking days we were totally selfish and we didn't really value anyone at all. We never properly experienced the fellowship of other human beings around us, or companionship of a personal nature, even if we were in a relationship. But now, our normal human instincts want the proper rewards of companionship. A single friend said to me recently that when he sometimes felt a little fearful, he wished he could go home and explain it to someone close to him, and that person would be on his side, hold him and tell him it will be alright. We are all a bit childlike, especially us alcoholics, and maybe this is a bit like getting reassurance from a parent. But whatever it really is, we miss it when we can't have it.

Other parts of normal living, like spare time and holidays, making a home and bringing up kids all benefit hugely from close companionship. The fellowship of AA is not designed to support these directly – a good relationship is the best solution for such things.

We Want Romance

Why do so many people like to read romance novels and watch romantic movies? If you do a search about Amazon book earnings, you'll see that romance authors earn around 170% more than other writers. If you read some of those books (or watch romantic movies), you can see how they're aimed at our instinctive desire to have that humorous, light hearted and trouble free romance with a happy ending. Notice interestingly though, that a lot of those books and films are about people 'finding themselves', followed by a personality change – how they were at the start of the story is not (by some easy miracle) how they are at the end.

They straighten up and fly right and then form a trusting, deep, perfect romance and live happily ever after. It's not like that for us.

But what is romance? It doesn't seem to serve any great purpose for the instincts of life does it? If we look at the basic dictionary definition we find it says romance is a feeling of excitement and mystery associated with love, or that it's love which is sentimental or idealised. Or, that romance is a type of love affair, especially one that is not very serious or long-lasting. Those are not really satisfactory descriptions to me. It's a bit like we soon find we don't have adequate definitions of other words such as humility – we know that humility has an extensive breadth of meaning, far beyond just behaving in a humble way.

If romance was really quite frivolous, sentimental and idealistic, why then is it given so much central thought in peoples' minds? What I mean is, if it was relatively meaningless, I and millions of other people would be bored stiff after one or two rom-com movies or romantic novels yet as the statistics show, many people have a big appetite for the stuff. I myself have a constant desire for some romance, I think it is one of the essential elements of a happy life. I can't imagine a relationship without some romantic times; a walk hand in hand, a quiet dinner for two or a hug under a blanket watching a movie. These little elements of romance are to me, essential, and part of the rewards of a relationship.

Like anything though, it has to be in balance. Many people keep seeking romance in a destructive way, perhaps moving from relationship to relationship, desperately trying to find that perfect romance - maybe like an addiction or obsession. Again, in that context, it doesn't sound at all trivial. Anyway, we'll get to the problems of being overly romantic later in the book, but I think for now, if we are saying we want good relationships, then we want some romance in there.

We Want/Need Sex?

Do we need sex in a relationship? Oh boy, there's a question. And one to which most men answer yes and a lot of women answer no. Of course that's a bit simplistic, but in essence, about right. The sex drive as it's called out there, or the sex instinct as we would call it, is a powerful yet fickle thing. When it comes down to it, I personally believe that a good relationship needs an appropriate element of sex. If a relationship doesn't, it can be a very difficult battle keeping it stable and happy.

There may be occasions when sex is not possible, with illness for example. At these times partners usually cope fine because there's a practical reason why sex cannot happen and so it's easily accepted by our instincts.

But I think we should put this a different way. What our sex instinct really does not need is to be out of balance and the problem here is that sex requires two people – so our sex instinct is dependent on someone else for that balance. The amount of sex or type of sex is not the measure here, but how you and your partner are with both your sex instincts together and whether you both genuinely feel in a good balanced zone with your sex life. Understanding and contentment with regards to sex and the sex instinct is what we need.

We Want a Family

For this discussion we should separate the extended family from partners and children. And although we usually prioritise our immediate family as our highest concern, it's the extended family that forms the longest-running human relationship component in our lives.

WANTS, NEEDS, RISKS AND SITUATIONS

Most of us, if we're lucky, still have our parents and siblings. We should understand that they are one of the major mechanisms that made us what we are. Grandparents, aunties and uncles may also have had an important part to play in the development of our character. Our lives as children, and on into adulthood, were a complex web of both effective and ineffective learning, good and bad emotional processes, and a history of pain and joy. All these things weave in and out of us, through all our actions and responses – and into our alcoholism. Add to that how we independently developed into self-driven people and we find a very complicated picture of our own personalities. Understanding all this is, of course, one of the core tasks of the steps. [by the way, if you're new to recovery, don't feel disheartened at this prospect – as recovering alcoholics we are among a very small number of people who actually get a chance to unravel all this stuff].

We learn that when we stop drinking, one of our early tasks is to make amends to our families simply by improving our behaviour. Bit-by-bit we react less and become more accepting. Making amends to our family in this way is one of those essential types of loving things that's a core part of God's will for us. When I have an awkward family situation and ask for his will for me, the answer is always clearly about patience and courage and not to try and defend or justify myself. Then somehow it becomes attraction rather than promotion, just gently doing the right thing slowly builds their trust, and having other peoples' trust is one of the few things that we can safely use to build our self-esteem. As they say, if you want esteem, do esteem-able things – and nowhere does this apply more than in our actions towards family members.

So, getting on to the the issue of having our own family, do we really need a family at all? You could logically argue that we don't. But what is a good relationship if it's not also a family in a sense? Even if we don't have kids, should a long-term relationship remain on the same footing as it is in early dating, or should it take on some of the form of a family? Well I for one think it should, because I don't see how it can be spiritually balanced if it does not. Thus, when debating the issue of wanting a relationship then I also think that means we should want a family. I think here, family infers the correct level of responsibility we should bring to a personal relationship. We can't treat one person we're in a relationship with, with any less responsibility than we should a family.

Risks

Risk is the possibility of something bad happening. Something gets increasingly risky as either the likelihood of it happening increases or the effect from it happening becomes less and less desirable. As alcoholics we were incredibly high risk-takers. Each and every one of our character defects and bad actions had so much risk that, inevitably, many of them did end in whatever predictably undesirable outcome they were sure to bring. You know the expression "the yet's"? This or that horrible thing hasn't happened to us *yet* – that's our sort of risk.

And maybe "it works if you work it" is our risk-reduction plan.

The Biggest Relationship Risk is Lack of Wisdom

When it comes to relationships the biggest risk is this – we don't know enough about them. When we start our recoveries, we don't know anything useful about living any part of our lives. The Fellowship starts us off in the right direction, lifting us up from total insanity and points us at a spiritual life. It covers so many of our own internal defects such as our self will, dishonesty, lack of humility and so-on. And it takes us into the realm of service and fellowship. But it doesn't say much about safely bedding a lover.

A lot of people are fearful of discussing a large part of the relationship spectrum, particularly in the areas of desire, jealousy and sexual behaviour. And there are some rather funny attitudes and sayings around AA about relationships. You might hear useful or stupid comments in equal measure, and they vary whether from the mouths of men or women. "Up every skirt is a slip", I heard one guy say. And I heard a woman say she'd never get into another relationship because all men want is "to control women". People say "don't start a relationship in the first year of sobriety" – maybe that one is useful. But only on the odd occasion might you hear people talk with depth about relationships, and then often with apprehension – as if the topic is largely off limits in the Fellowship for some reason.

In essence this is crazy. I said the problem was a lack of wisdom, exactly the sort of wisdom we mean at the end of the serenity prayer. The fellowship works so hard to build up our wisdom in other areas so what I'm suggesting is that we copy the process with regard to relationships. Talk about it more, develop our knowledge and useful experiences more, share about it more and sponsor about it more.

Some might say this is not related to alcoholism. I disagree. Bill W wrote about the family afterwards as a starting point I think. And to me, any normal aspect of life that risks my sobriety, that my alcoholism can use as an excuse for me to pick up a drink, absolutely should be part of my program.

The Risk of In-love and Romance

We want lots of love and romance, that's what we identified a little earlier in this chapter. But in-love is a damn hazard as well, if we're not careful.

I've seen quite a few people in AA, and I include myself in this, go into relationships in totally the wrong way, for the wrong reasons and without any awareness of the risks. And I've seen people who are in long-term relationships where a lot of things have gone wrong, blinded to the problems because of the in-love feelings.

It's the classic "fools rush in where wise men fear to tread". Speaking bluntly, you could say men are led by their dicks and women lay honey traps. Crude expressions but ones that we know ring true so many times. And we alcoholics fantasise with overblown egos about a perfect romance or an amazing sexual conquest – and we're suckers for anything that might be a quick fix. Passion, lust, falling hopelessly in love, all a drug according to some scientists who say these things release endorphins in the brain. That's why we have to watch out, because chasing tail can be addictive.

So through the book, one of my aims is to keep an eye out for all the hazards and temptations, and make sure we understand them. It's so important to see the truth with desires for relationships just like with any other things in our lives that we might not be responsible enough to deal with.

The Unmanageability Risk

When we first come into the rooms we are aware that our lives are unmanageable. We know alcohol is destroying us yet we can't stop drinking it. And we probably know we are at rock-bottom and that this mess is not an outcome of effective management (effective management being a crude opposite of unmanageability).

In my drinking days, I would think about alcohol all the time – even when I was not drinking it. When I was at work I was always wondering what time I would finish and thus get my hands on a drink. My unmanageability was almost total, and of course I thought it was everyone else's fault, particularly my partner's at the time.

I remember one very good piece of advice given to me, and it was given quite forcefully. I asked someone "why is my life unmanageable" the answer that was fired straight back was "because you're trying to manage it" And later this proved to be so true with the problem of relationships. If you look honestly at yourself you might find that as well as managing your own life badly, you're managing a partner's life badly too.

Living with lots of unmanageability, whether drinking or sober, creates a wake of problems. The reason is, when we're unmanageable neither we, or those people around us, make decisions for the right reasons. And, by the way, it's important to remember some of our past decisions might later turn out to be right by dumb luck, not good judgement. We have to be honest about this so that we don't believe we're good at making decisions on our own. We're not.

Or maybe we suffer from a serious lack of emotional sobriety, or we're afflicted by that type of self-will run riot where we just don't know what we need, what's right or good for us, and seem to rapidly change our minds and make very poor choices. In essence we're unknowingly driven by our out-of-balance instincts. And when we're in this condition it's often relationship problems that are the next biggest driver of unmanageability after liquor.

Manageability comes from doing our recovery program of course, and I suppose the purpose of this book is to try and bring that manageability to our relationships. These things take time and a lot of work but for now I'm just really reminding ourselves that the unmanageability aspect of step one must be taken very seriously when it comes to relationships.

Life Situations

I think it's important to define different types of life and relationship situations that we might be in. I'm aiming to cover most of the major scenarios but if you have other specific details then you should define your own situation with clarity.

Relationship has Failed

Sometimes when people get into recovery they find that their current relationship is no longer viable. For the majority of us it's largely our fault of course – we were so bad in our drinking days that the in-love feeling that our partner once had for us, is gone. This could be a complicated situation, with children involved, a family home and so-on, so significant unmanageability to deal with. It's going to be a time when you need to go to lots of meetings, keep close to your recovery buddies and talk a lot with your sponsor. If your relationship is dead and there is no way to repair it, you're going to have to move on. You have to face that you can't fix it and whilst that might be extremely painful, this is one of those big things that you need to accept you cannot change. And you must be careful not to let your situation, and perhaps your angry partner's behaviour, undermine your sobriety.

Or maybe it's you that feels your relationship has come to an end. When you start to get sober there's so much change in you, including better clarity, that it might be you that realises that you don't love your partner, or that the relationship is too dysfunctional for you now. Usually both people are damaged in an alcoholic relationship, and when one seeks recovery, more imbalances in the other person become apparent. We can see that the relationship was never based on proper love or sensible reasons to be together, so it cannot function now when one of us gets sober.

It's a particularly strange irony, this particular type of ending of a relationship, when both of you were heavy drinkers. You seemed to be functioning when you were both drinking, but can't when one of you gets sober. You have to accept that you are changing for the better, and are having to work hard to find sobriety and make your life worth living again. The truth is, you may find you simply cannot stay in a badly dysfunctional relationship, especially if your partner is still drinking.

Relationship is Recoverable

The overall state of your relationship might be pretty bad, but there is hope of recovering it. If you are in early sobriety and you are gaining some genuine optimism, then it might be that those close around you start to have the same hopes – that maybe you are starting to get well again. At this time I think there are two main factors. First that you demonstrate, every day, that you are not going to pick up a drink again because this is the only thing that your loved-ones want to see right now. Chances are you've sworn off the drink many times before and let them down, so at first you have to understand that although they don't want you to, they're expecting you to fail. And second, you're going to need a lot of patience before you get any genuine affirmation from those around you that the AA recovery process has any real value.

It's probably during the first few months of recovery that you're going to see if the relationship is recoverable – and whether or not it's worth recovering. At this time, if things feel positive for you and your partner, even though it's going to be shaky, then you may be in a position to go forward in the relationship. There's going to be a lot of work to do, and if you have children there's all that to deal with as well.

In a Relationship for the Wrong Reasons

The chances of success or failure of a relationship is primarily dependent on honesty. We know that honesty is a non-negotiable requirement in recovery, and it's the same for relationships. Openness and honesty is difficult enough between two people when their underlying commitment is good, but a relationship based on something that is grossly dishonest is a very unhealthy thing.

Maybe you're with someone because they provide for your security instinct. Perhaps they earn good money or own the house you live in, but you don't have proper feelings for them. Or you're with someone because you've had children with them and you believe you should continue the relationship for the kid's sake, despite serious flaws in the relationship. And then there are much more risky scenarios, where people stay in dangerous relationships where abuse or violence occurs, but they don't have the courage to leave.

Another common problem is where you might be in a relationship with someone who's a heavy drinker, or has other addiction problems, yet this person always seems to understand you, even support you when you fall off the wagon. You justify the relationship when other people query it, by saying how your partner relates to your alcoholism. You think you would lose that sympathy if you finished the relationship. This is a very dangerous situation.

There are many more examples, but I think you get the point. You cannot expect to live a happy existence where a relationship is seriously dysfunctional. It can be a massive issue to resolve of course, particularly if there are major money problems to deal with or children involved. But with great care, humility and hard work, you can find a way out.

Can't Get Over a Past Relationship

One area that can be particularly troublesome is when a relationship has stopped but then later you feel it shouldn't have ended, so you want to start the relationship again. We can feel lonely and insecure at such times for practical reasons, but the big problem is when strong feelings of in-love for the other person keep coming back, even after the relationship has finished. And that love might not be reciprocated, or perhaps the relationship was badly dysfunctional, so it's not logical that you should want to start the relationship again. But those are the feelings you have even though it doesn't make any sense to you (or friends) why you want to get back together. We often say we feel a terrible loss and are heartbroken. And maybe these sorts of illogical feelings show just how much 'in-love' can be cunning, baffling and powerful.

On the other hand, sometimes relationships can re-start successfully. It might be that a couple have a break and make some important changes to themselves, then find they can make it successful later on. Again no cut-and-dried answers, just be aware of the difficulties of these situations.

Single Before and Now

Maybe you had relationships in the past, but towards the end of your drinking days you were single. And so, entering early recovery you are a single person. Or maybe you've been in recovery longer and either haven't had a relationship, or were unsuccessful with some relationships in early recovery.

One simple thing to say though, don't rush into relationships any more. We all go in too fast. People say don't have a relationship in recovery in the first year. In principle that's good advice – you just don't know enough about this new way of living to risk it too soon. And don't forget, the other person might be a bit bonkers too. Don't commit yourself without knowing what they're really like.

You're a Parent

If you have children, there are several important things to mention at this point. First of course, for any recovering alcoholic who has children, it's a simple fact that putting things right in that area is one of the longest, toughest and most emotional aspects of recovery. If you're reading this and you have kids, then I understand how you feel – I have two children (now in their twenties) and they went through the worst of my drinking and the collapse of their family. If things are bad for you at the moment then just take your time, hang on through the tough days and have hope because like everything else that comes from a twelve step recovery program, the promises will come regarding our children too.

You may still be in the relationship in which you had children and were drinking, or maybe your family is no longer together, either way you will of course be hoping to rebuild a good relationship with your kids. It's vitally important though that you don't carry massive guilt about the past with regards to your children. I was helped with this very early in my recovery, but I've seen other folk eaten-up with guilt and remorse about what their children went through and what it might mean for their future. It's a huge source of crippling fear for us if we're not very careful.

Bill W wrote an excellent essay on fear for Grapevine (the AA magazine) in 1961. In it he describes how we must do the best we can to remove as much fear as possible, then deal constructively with any fear that remains. Ask for help from your recovery buddies with this in the early days – reacting with lots of fear around your children is not good for your recovery and your children will pick up on it. And watch out not to make bad decisions about them out of fear.

And if you are still in a relationship with the other parent, any chance you might have to resurrect the in-love instinct with your partner may depend largely on mending your relationship with your children. Remember that it's not really about you in this situation – its a sober parent's natural defence mechanism to protect their children and you have been their greatest threat, and the cause of the other parent's greatest fear. It may be that your partner believes that the parental love between you and your children is worth fighting for and hence they carry on with you in their lives. Or maybe you have a period of separation whilst the dust settles. But if you have a strong programme you have a chance – and remember, a slip now is going to be a severe setback for all of you (no pressure).

And another little thing to remember, most kids love it if you as a parent are in a healthy stable relationship – whether with their other parent or another good adult. So building a good new relationship should also be seen as something important for them too. Don't make that too big a priority and force a new relationship for that reason, but keep it in mind as a good thing – it's part of the bridge to normal living. You may have heard the expression about giving children roots and wings, well even grown-up kids are comforted by the knowledge that they can come back to the roots of a parent in a stable relationship and loving home.

Chapter Three – Instincts

After I had been living sober for around three years, in my little apartment in mid-Wales, some basic change had happened to me. I'd got a lot fitter physically, I looked and dressed better, I was calmer – perhaps even a little bit cool maybe.

The little town where I lived was an old Victorian spa town. It used to be a retreat for Victorian gentlefolk and it's had very little development since that period, so it's very authentic. Every August they have a Victorian festival with music and markets and the local residents (and keen visitors) dress all week in Victorian garb. At the end of the week the town has an evening of fireworks and fairground attractions around the pretty lake that's there. So this particular year, half the town's population and I (on my own) went up to the lake for the evening's festivities. I walked around the stalls, watched a few street entertainers, then stood for a while as children went "ooh" at the fireworks. And I was in a bit of a dream state – a strange combination of people-watching and meditation. It was much like you might do in early recovery the first time you walk around a garden and take in the beauty of the flowers; realising you hadn't done anything like that all those years you were drinking.

Well that's what I found myself doing at the lake that night. I became aware that no one was really drinking much liquor from the two or three cider stalls that were there, families were playing and laughing quietly and with good manners, couples were holding hands or hugging each other in the now chilly air. They were looking handsome, looking content, looking as splendid as flowers in a lovely garden. I felt pretty sad about all this. It showed me very starkly how my previous world had been so distorted, my single-minded obsession for drink blinding me from all this life. I remember thinking, "Damn, I want to live properly in this world now and have a lovely relationship that functions wholly within this beauty, not the mess of pain and unmanageability that I had created before."

As I then progressed further through my recovery, doing inventories, trying to get honest, trying to find humility and faith, I also started to find more of the promises coming my way. Friendships, improvements in my business, regular walks in the countryside, taking in a musical show, some fitness and other good stuff. And then I wondered if I could have romance.

Looking back at that night at the lake, I can see that my instincts were starting to come together. In my drinking days any natural instincts were hugely out of balance, or even non-existent – they certainly were not functioning as God intended. But maybe now things could change.

The Basic Instincts of Life According to AA

The concept that we are driven by three basic instincts of life is one of the foundations of our recovery program. In the Big Book it lays out the idea that we have the security, social and sex instincts. We learn how the actions of every human being is driven by these three instincts. The saint or the kind nurse, devout mother or charity worker probably have these instincts in good balance. Murderers and tyrants – clearly not. And of course people who are lost in life find it hard to live with correctly balanced instincts, such as those with addictions, phobias, depression or reckless egos.

INSTINCTS

In essence the three instincts determine how we look after ourselves, or not, as the case may be. The security instinct includes basics such as food and water, clothing and a roof over our heads. The social instinct covers aspects such as our need to socialise with other human beings and have companionship. And the sex instinct is there so that we reproduce the species. And it's easy to see that all three of these would play a significant part in any successful relationship.

But what is meant by having instincts that are in or out of balance? Well we can easily start with plenty of out-of-balance examples by looking back at our own drinking days. We didn't provide for ourselves properly, we had no proper drive to keep a job or keep a tidy house or wash our clothes. We clearly risked the security of our health by drinking. Maybe we isolated ourselves away from people, or maybe we wanted to be the life and soul of every party, trying too hard to be liked. And were we not reckless in our sex lives – behaving promiscuously and hurting other people for selfish sexual gratification, or becoming delinquent in the maintenance of a proper sex-life with a once loving partner?

But do we really know what the full spectrum of each instinct might be? And where do we sit on the scale for each instinct, good or bad? Of course, the way we acquire knowledge of ourselves in this respect is by doing steps four and five. And when identified we then work towards the correct levels in these instincts through steps six, seven and ten.

Not living with instincts properly in balance is a major humility problem in my view, and a spiritual thing also – if you are truly in the sunlight of the spirit you cannot have badly out of balance instincts.

The Security Instinct

There are, I'm sure, very many aspects of the security instinct – a huge number of different ways this instinct could be in or out of balance. So I'm only going to mention a few here that might be useful in the context of relationships.

A relationship is a highly emotional thing. So I think emotional security needs to be a key part of a good relationship. But what is emotional security and how do you provide that to a partner? A useful way to understand this is actually to take a look at how children need and respond to emotional security (credit to my wife for coming up with this one). As a parent, or other responsible adult around children, there are things we learn we should and should not do. We shouldn't mock children, undermine them, embarrass them in front of strangers. We should have lots of patience, hugs when they need it and gentle, long-term discipline (with even more patience). We should bring spontaneity, humour and our own resilience when things go wrong. Calmness and consistency, tolerance, kindness and love, all delivered with completely genuine intentions. Our old alcoholic behaviour of manipulation, false promises, unreliability and so-on just won't do. So, all these things, good and bad, are the keys to the emotional security of those people who are dependent upon us.

And then of course the mechanics of safe living are important for a good relationship. Financial instability very quickly destroys security, as does problems with jobs and housing. If a relationship also includes children then the requirement for security is even greater in this regard. But we must, as alcoholics, take our time in these areas – plan carefully but try not to rush, and gently put measures in place to increase the structure of security around ourselves. All of this may not seem romantic directly of course, but put it the other way round; living in fear about our security is not a turn-on.

The Social Instinct

The social instinct is perhaps more fickle and difficult to understand than the other two instincts. But I was surprised when I discovered just how important this instinct is, and how its significance is both less easy to see, yet far more of a factor than is first apparent.

We're all very aware of our past social problems – in our drinking days we were totally selfish with our extreme social demands, and just plain antisocial as far as everyone else was concerned. I for one was the sort of alcoholic who demanded lots of social attention - at least until I was too drunk to care.

Then as we move into sobriety we tend to do two clearly related things with our social interactions – we usually stop socialising with our drinking buddies and start socialising with our recovery buddies. The primary reason of course is that it's far easier to keep away from booze this way. But there are even more important aspects of this instinct for genuine wellbeing I think.

Firstly, we should consider how human beings mimic other people. Right from early childhood, we would copy or mimic the behaviour of others – and sometimes not in a good way. Then, as we grew into alcoholics, we would rapidly align with other extreme or rebellious characters around us. But now, in sobriety, we start to make friends for very different reasons. Safety is one for sure, and genuine friendship, but we might not be so aware that the most important reason is to learn.

Like a child who copies older friends or siblings, spending time now with healthier people rubs off on us. We see that we want to be like those people who have good sobriety and good relationships. We listen and learn from what they say and do. One of our basic sayings is "we have to become teachable". This of course requires the genuine acceptance that we might be wrong, that someone else might be right, and that putting into practice the examples they show us will be better than anything we can come up with on our own. Doing this repeatedly, so that we practice the process, is critical – it's useless listening and nodding at our friends' support and guidance, yet not doing it. Indeed, if you can't take advice from a few good friends then I think you're going to struggle to work effectively with a sponsor.

So this is how socialising brings one clear and direct benefit to us – it's so important to our ongoing development and wellbeing. However, (I wonder if you can see this one coming?), we must be careful that a relationship does not push out this necessary process. Some social learning can be done together as a couple but not all of it. As individuals we need to spend time with our buddies. The men with their mates, the girls with their girlfriends, sponsors with sponsees, sisters with sisters and brothers with brothers. And partners should respect each other's needs with this. Wanting all your partner's time, always wanting to be with your partner when they're seeing friends, or worse, even being jealous about it, just won't work. Hopefully, with my explanation here, it will be easier for partners to accept this as a genuinely important need.

And, as our recovery improves, so our social skills move in the right direction too. I guess social skills are really the same thing as the principles we learn in the steps, particularly those good things that have a positive impact on people around us. And as we learn to accept support from our friends, we also learn how to give that support back to them. If we give them good advice, and our friends lives improve, then that's a very estimable thing – we get genuine self esteem from it and we gain similar spiritual development as we do when helping other alcoholics.

Then logically this behaviour will have a positive impact on family and partners. If we are socially mature and responsible with friends, and learn from them, we can bring that back into our personal relationships. And whilst I said don't crowd-out your partner and their friends, you should be involved with those friendships to the correct degree. And watch out you are not over-indulging in certain aspects of your own friendships to the detriment of your partner's wellbeing – examples we all see are some men's obsession for discussing sports with their mates or some women's excessive desire to debate child-raising and home-building topics.

The Sex Instinct

In early recovery we have to be very careful with our emerging instincts, because we're not qualified to use them at this point. We look back and see the hazards of making bad choices, so now we ask our recovery buddies and sponsor to help us with decisions. However, if the need for a decision comes from our deeper instincts we still tend to not ask for help. We are frightened of discussing those deeper feelings – and because of this, the raw sex instinct in particular can become a big hazard.

We probably don't remember too much about our other instincts from our drinking days, but usually do recall some of our crazy sex exploits, such as stupid flings or one-night stands. These events then become shrouded in a lot of fear and guilt. And then in sobriety, the sex instinct can kick-in very strongly. Remember it's designed for reproduction of the species so, beyond all else, it's what we're programmed to do. At the end of our drinking days we were probably so ineffective and in such a bad state that we weren't having sex. But now, the sudden possibility of real sex, sex that could be so exciting and laden with heady physical fulfilment, can very quickly cause havoc again. It's a risky time because this powerful urge can outweigh our efforts to better manage our lives. Be patient, we're aiming for good sustainable results. Rushing into bed with the first willing person we might find is not a good idea.

So it's vitally important in recovery, and in relationships, to properly discuss and understand the sex instinct – not doing so is a big mistake. I hear many people in the rooms make unpleasant or negative comments, turn away, or quickly change the subject when the topic of sex comes up. But you have to take it on, and learn about it. Not learning about the sex instinct is as foolish as not reading The Doctor's Opinion in my view. You've got to know what you're working with (no seedy jokes please).

Oh, a note on thirteen stepping again. I think men are more likely to initiate an inappropriate approach towards a woman because of the obvious 'sex' part of the sex instinct. But when I ask women about their experiences, they find they fall into the thirteen step trap because of the desire for reassurance that after their terrible drinking days they might be a viable partner again, in essence to validate their sexuality but maybe not for sex itself.

Is There Really an In-love Instinct?

In chapter one I outlined how there may be such a thing as a fourth instinct – the in-love instinct. The example I gave in chapter two was based on the considerable hurt we feel if a partner we love ends the relationship. And at the start of this chapter I described what felt like an unsatisfied instinct as I walked around that lake in Wales. I felt some sort of gap, as if something was missing, yet I couldn't really see how the usual three basic instincts were the ones suffering. I just wanted the feeling that I believed would only come from a romantic relationship.

INSTINCTS

Let's look at our general interaction with other people. We want to be around people and have fellowship with people partly because of the social instinct. But we also want fellowship for security – certainly when it comes to our fellows in AA because we hope we are going to learn from them how to live sober – they are the crew and passengers on our sinking ship. And we get some of our social and security needs met in a similar way from family members, work colleagues and friends.

Next, we carry out all the mating ritual stuff – chatting-up people and flirting because of the sex instinct. But flirting is not the same as romance, because it doesn't trigger the same feelings. If someone is being flirtatious just for sex and gets turned down, they quickly move on to the next potential conquest. But where there is in-love forming, the consequence of rejection is much more significant. So it seems to me that the romantic, in-love feeling and whether it's an instinct or not, is a worthy debate – if for no other reason than to force us to think about it all.

There are many forms of love that we often discuss in the rooms. There's love for the planet and the beauty of our surroundings, or love for our parents, siblings, children and animals. And there's love for our comrades in arms, the sick and needy, and the people we try and help in the fellowship. Then there are the concepts of love itself to understand – the love that we might have been taught about from the Bible, where love is patient, love is kind...

But none of these things are the same as the instinctual drive for affection, companionship and intimacy that can only be obtained from a personal relationship. Why for example, do we passionately kiss a partner whom we're in-love with (or might be a prospect for in-love) yet would never kiss any other individual in that way?

When a proper romantic partnership starts to form, in the early days there will be some friendship, common interests and so on. Then one or both persons will start to take a stronger interest in the other – the other person's existence becomes somehow amplified as the in-love instinct kicks in.

And if the in-love instinct does exist, we should accept that it is powerful and treat it with respect. For example, as a relationship develops, both people need be very careful about the increasing emotional reliance that each is building in the other, and thus the greatly increasing responsibility each must take for the other. We hear in the rooms "we are responsible", and in my view, never more so than in a personal relationship. In particular, this responsibility must surely be focussed on our own steps six, seven and ten – it's our unresolved defects that could form the basis of future harms to the other person.

I've spoken with many people about their painful experiences in relationships. Of course there were many examples of relationships breaking down because of violence, cheating, financial irresponsibility or just drunkenness. And I asked people what the damage felt like, what was their experience as they got out of the relationship. The answers were of course about the carnage, the resentments, and hatred even, but also in some examples a deep sense of loss, not for sex, but for the in-love they once had.

But we also know that instincts are there to serve a purpose – they are a driver for the survival of the species. But what's the role of the in-love instinct in survival? Could it be that it's the drive that achieves the strongest love of another human being possible – so that we are prepared to put the other person's wellbeing, or even life, first. It's much more than brotherly love or love of our fellows, and of course very different from our love of God.

It seems to me that the social and security instincts major on self-preservation. The sex instinct is there for the continuation of our genetic code and thus focussed on the preservation of our children. Perhaps the in-love instinct is primarily there for the preservation of someone other than ourselves or our children. It's a fourth element of protection for the family unit across three generations that brings a greater depth of resilience by carrying forward critical knowledge and wisdom. The in-love instinct provides protection for our partners from early dating right through to old age. I also think it's connected to how marriage is recognised by God. We don't always understand the will of our higher power, but I'm sure that part of his will for me is to take good care of my wife.

Later on in the book, I expand the processes and mechanisms related to the in-love instinct considerably. But I'll say one critical thing right now – you should remember that the balance of your in-love instinct is dependent on your partner's sanity and spiritual condition just as much as theirs is on yours.

Other Animal Instincts

Humans clearly have quite a few one-level-down instincts that lie below the surface of our major traits. They still fall under the main instincts but maybe are a bit more 'animal' in their characteristics. Some of these are strong, like the fight or flight instinct we have when faced with a sudden dangerous threat, others are small yet detailed behaviours. And beware, they are different in men and women. Sometimes they're good, like the child caring instinct in a woman or the bread winning instinct in a man, and sometimes not so good like the instinct in men to spread their seed (and cheat) or the instinct in women to obtain the best seed (and cheat). Now, don't panic about me mentioning cheating like this – I say this to emphasise how things that are clearly right or wrong, can be undermined by natures intended instincts. Infidelity is something that crosses the path of most of our lives at some point and whilst the drivers are to some extent understandable, their effect is so damaging that our fundamental requirement not to cause harm should override such behaviour (and infidelity is one of those classic instinct-based faults that just a few drinks will elevate to command status).

The development of instincts is an evolutionary mechanism of course, passed down in the genes of all creatures. I was watching a TV program some time ago about penguins and how, once the female has laid an egg, the male takes sole responsibility to look after the egg and keep it warm until it hatches. Apparently a female penguin will not do this task at all – she does not possess that instinct, nor can she learn how to do it. And if the male fails in his duties, the female will stand there, aware of the seriousness of the problem but totally unable to keep the egg warm. The human male and female differences are all there too – some obvious and some not so. My partner and I have looked at specific examples within ourselves, one being jobs around the house (a common one for us all). It's easy to criticise each other, saying how we don't see eye-to-eye, or one of us is more enthusiastic than the other about something, or one of us likes things to be done a different way to the other. But looking more deeply we can sometimes see that our difference of capability might be like the penguins'. Kathryn accepts that I can't change a duvet cover as quickly or as easily as she can, and I accept that she can't quickly work out why a cupboard door won't close properly, even though the cause of the problem is straightforward (to me). We just don't seem to be equally equipped in these areas.

How about a different idea – that sex and fighting are linked? They often are in the animal kingdom. Male herd animals will fight other males for the dominant position and the right to mate with the females of the herd. Young men will often chase girls in pubs and night clubs (usually alcohol fuelled of course) and sometimes fight over them. This is, presumably, an instinct to establish rites and boundaries between the men, and then get to mate with the best girls – even though their judgement of best might be based on irrelevant evidence such as how good the girl's makeup is or how short her skirt. Of course the instinct of the girls has an effect too – she want to mate with the strongest male, so the ensuing fight between the guys is an exhibition of who is the best prospect for fathering her children. This scenario might seem quite stupid but I'm sure many alcoholics can see plenty of this stuff somewhere in their inventory.

Here's another interesting aspect of sex and fighting, but it's more to do with the vainglory of tribal feuding, or even warfare. One rainy evening a few years ago I was playing one of those shoot-em-ups on a game console. This particular game involves shooting lots of aliens and sometimes meeting up with your own human soldiers and fighting as a unit, using big vehicles with all sorts of guns on board to go killing the alien enemy. Sometimes I enjoyed the game and sometimes I didn't so much – occasionally finding the tension of it all rather unsettling. But later that day when I went to bed I had a sort of half-dream that I was one of the soldiers riding a huge battle vehicle with my comrades, all of us firing wildly at our enemy. But it felt very different. Now I was really glad to be there with those other guys and we were fighting to protect our world, our race – and our girls back home. They say girls love a man in uniform, and war is often romanticised as being something good in that respect (even though we know it's not). But it's definitely there – men's instinct to fight warfare based on not only the security instinct but the sex instinct too. These days, this particular combination of instinctual behaviours is probably translated into the supporting of sports such as football that clearly generate similar feelings of instinctual comradeship and heightened sexuality.

Communication Instincts

Our communication processes are partly instinctual too I think. Most creatures have communication instincts – bees dance, ants rub antennae, whales sing. Humans have the spoken and written word but also facial expressions, body language and pheromones.

So if we are going to improve communication within relationships we should be mindful that sometimes communication is instinct driven. For example, raising our voice when our security instinct is threatened, or the opposite, going quiet when our security instinct is threatened (aggression reaction or fear reaction). 'Bigging-up' and bullshitting to bolster our social instinct, or the opposite again, talking timidly to bolster the social instinct (winning friends by playing the sympathy card). And of course, behaving in a loud and brash manner, or on the other hand, talking coyly (you might say acting coquettishly) is often used for the sex instinct.

There are other factors too. Different races, ethnic groups, religious groups, class groups and even different families have big variations in the way they communicate. And sometimes we instinctively group our style of communication for social acceptance by copying or mimicking, such as with regional dialect and accents. And then there's the issue of communication habits – some of us are prone to disapproving facial expressions, or getting too close into someones personal space, or not appearing to listen, and so-on.

So have a good think and discussion about your communication instincts. You might be surprised what you find there.

The Balance of Our Instincts

We talk all the time about balance in recovery. Too much or too little of anything is probably best avoided. The number of meetings we go to, how much literature we read, how much exercise we take – all things in early recovery we start to think about. But there are other important things to sort out too. Finding somewhere decent to live for example, is part of improving the balance of our security instinct.

But we're focussing on relationships here and the big question is, can some of the major parts of our instincts ever be in balance if we're not in a good relationship? And if not, how far out of balance might that put us? Two years ago I lost a fellowship friend who died unexpectedly from a massive stroke. And as fate had it, we had spent five days together on a spiritual retreat on Caldey Island (Wales) only the week before, and during our long walks together he told me he so deeply wished he was in a relationship. You could feel the loneliness - a constant level of emotional pain within him. And because I was writing this book, I think I was one of only a very few people with whom he ever shared those feelings. I think his pain was the consequence of his in-love instinct being out of balance.

And then there's the balance of our sex instinct. If we're not in a good relationship then apart from opting for some rather unsavoury choices, I think we can say our sex instinct is out of balance. Now, I don't really know how bad it is if our sex instinct is out of balance – it certainly feels bad to me, but we're not all the same. I think some of us will be subtly out of adjustment and others might be significantly destabilised if this instinct is not in good balance.

So, whilst we go deeply into the security and social instincts in our programmes of recovery, I don't think most of us will examine our in-love and sex instincts very well. You could reasonably say that many of us only do work on fifty percent of the major instinct driven characteristics that effect us. To me that's far too much of a gap – certainly it would be for my recovery and my marriage.

Develop Your Own Instinct – for Instincts

An increasing awareness of our instincts starts in early recovery because we find instinct-related things on our inventory. Maybe it's how we might react excessively when a particular part of an instinct is threatened. We look at the defect and often find the root cause in an instinct – a fear for example that might stem back to an insecurity from our childhood. And as our inventory builds, we start to see how so many of our defects are based in out of balance instincts.

But when it comes to the issue of instincts and relationships we find that when we get close to another human being at a deep personal level, the effects, and faults, of instincts often become stronger.

In this chapter I have outlined what I think are the important issues regarding instincts, but the work doesn't stop here. Through the rest of the book you will find a great many examples and suggestions that have an instinct element to them. But now we have discussed them here, I'm sure you will always spot the instinctive part of any defect, problem, issue – or wonderful opportunity.

Chapter Four – Man-Brain Woman-Brain

We all accept that men and women are different, at the most basic level. But can we define those differences to some useful degree? I think so. It's a massive topic of course and there's no way I can do more than scratch the surface in this book – and it's only my opinion from my own experiences (and those few people who have helped me).

The expressions 'man-brain' and 'woman-brain' have been used by many people, you'll find lots of discussion on the web for example. Some say it's scientifically proven that our brains are physically different, others say it's not proven at all. Some believe it's religious doctrine and some say it's all caused by growing-up in our seriously gender-based society. But if we don't learn about these differences, wherever they come from, they can be the source of many misunderstandings, arguments and resentments.

In my relationship now, when we have the occasional misunderstanding, we see that some are caused by our basic character defects, differences of opinion or family backgrounds, but others are clearly based on differences in perception and interpretation that we can identify as male or female. And we often see these differences amplified or twisted in our cultures, particularly in TV and films. There are some very good books written on the subject of course – I've read two that were incredibly helpful and you might wish to check some out yourself (see References).

For most alcoholics, one of the first things to realise is that our own development as human beings was probably pretty slow in our early lives, and then in our drinking days it became virtually stagnant. I don't think many active alcoholics become wiser over the years. You'll sometimes hear people in AA sum up recovery as growing up. Growing-up applies to the core lessons to keeping sober for sure, but if you're now looking at your relationship prospects, then one of the gaps in your knowledge will be how 'man brain' and 'woman brain' work. You'll need to accept that at the start you'll be pretty useless at understanding both yourself, and the opposite sex in this regard.

One thing to mention here is the problem of inequality for men and women in our different lives and different societies. Sometimes inequality is real, and sometimes it's imagined in my experience. Sometimes it's just another one of those topics that the media like to stir up, and sometimes there really are unacceptable inequalities. But we shouldn't get confused between equality and same – men and women are not the same. We know what many of the bad examples of inequality might be out there of course. There are male bosses who might respectfully hold a door open for a woman employee, yet pay her less than her male counterpart. There are pretty women who trick or manipulate men for gain by flirting – or worse. Bad personal behaviour is rife in our society and it affects us on both a small and large scale – everywhere.

So for us, when we try to apply all that is good in our recovery principles, it means we should treat each other, men and women, in a wholly positive and constructive way, but also with full recognition of our differences.

Hunter or Nest-Builder

I like to imagine how some of our basic differences might come from our ancient lives. Men went hunting in packs and women stayed behind in the caves, raising children.

Men developed good navigational skills and talked little to keep quiet whilst tracking down their prey. They looked to each other to be cunning and brave, and relied on each other for their ability to successfully hunt as a team. Women made their caves warm and safe for giving birth and raising babies. The women talked loud and fast over the noise of the children, sharing all the intricacies of safe food preparation and nurturing the young. At the end of the day the men would light the fires and the women would cook the food. Maybe there would be some entertainment by dancing around the fires and beating drums. Then the men and women would go to their beds, under their animal skins.

And as they have sex, I can imagine their feelings about it – the women have been in company all day, with the affection of their children, whilst the men have had a more isolated day, and maybe been in some danger. The man wants the sexual release of tension, the feeling of the gentle female body against his, and the feeling of bonding. The woman gets turned on maybe by the masculinity of her mate, his strength and scent. She forgets for a while the myriad demands and problems of the day.

Okay, just daft images really, but you get the idea. You can paint your own pictures of the developing issues. Many differences formed out of the necessity of those lives, and I can imagine the clashes between the men and women as a result, even back in those early days. Maybe the men get up in the morning and are single-mindedly just thinking about the day's hunt and leave the cave in a mess. The women complain at this because it's impacting the careful cleaning regime in the cave, but the men don't see the reason for such a fuss. The women scream in fear at a mouse that has entered the cave – their baby's safety might be at risk but the men laugh at such panic, "it's only a tiny mouse and we're out there chasing buffalo!"

Ancient Pride and Modern Perception

We know from recovery that pride is a problem for us. Too much pride and an over-inflated ego are the enemy of being right-sized and having good humility. Uncontrolled pride leads us to tread on the toes of others and make bad decisions.

Looking back at our ancestors again, we can assume that the men formed pride for their skill in hunting and the women formed pride for their skill in raising children. The men's pride about hunting might lead to an unnecessary fight between two young men boasting who is better (despite a plea for calm from the women). Or worse, the men stir up conflict with adjacent villages, justifying it with the false honour of the hunter (that is building into the dangerous pride of the warrior). The women's pride in raising children might become competitive about the way the cave and kids are kept clean. Perhaps one of the women in the group doesn't come up to scratch in that department and the other women resent it.

So with regard to the differences between men and women, again it's useful to look back at our imaginary cave-dwelling lives, to think where our problem of pride originate from. In fact, I think this is critically important so I'll state it like this – the mechanisms of pride are different between men and women, and this results in major clashes between the sexes. A test you might like to try is think about some of the simple things you are prideful about, that are mostly the interests of your gender only –

and track it back over thousands of years. For men it might be that your team has just beaten a rival team in a critical football match (prideful warrior), or women it might be the beautiful baby clothes that you have just bought for your baby (prideful mother). Then think about how your interests in such matters don't align, and how you can feel hurt when your partner is not interested. That's what we call hurt pride of course. And just as pride is a problem when we inflict it on others, it's also a problem when others hurt our pride. So it's bad two ways.

Your perception of things often come from 'man brain' or 'woman brain' thinking, and they're not the same. There are many clichéd examples of this; women can't read maps or give directions, men can't find things in kitchen cupboards, women always want to 'talk about it' and men gaze into fires. And to my frustration, I sometimes really can't find things in a cupboard, only to be laughed at by Kathryn when she comes up and takes the particular item I was looking for right off the front of the shelf. My short-distance perception (around the cave) isn't very good.

Serial or Parallel Processing?

One of the main effects of how our male and female brains developed is the general way in which we seem to process our thinking. We always hear how women can multi-task and men cannot, or how women's brains have all their thinking processes running and connected to each other at the same time. And men only single-task – operating only one thinking process at a time, and needing to finish and shut down that process before starting the next one.

Probably, for women in the cave, allowing distraction to be registered and processed was important for raising lots of kids safely, whereas for a man out hunting dangerous prey, the slightest mental distraction could result in failure or even death. They are both strong survival mechanisms and a central element to the security instinct so we need to take these differences seriously, respecting them and working with them.

A word of warning about dominant same sex groups in families or places of work. If, for example a family is predominantly female then the female multi-tasking thinking will be dominant. This will seem natural to the women and amplified because this is a domestic environment. One or two men in that family group will struggle with interaction and even might feel ganged-up upon or criticised for not doing things right. Judgement and prejudice can soon follow if we don't stand back and understand what the truth of the situation is - and what real loving action is required. Or the other classic example, a predominantly male group in a place of work. Here, single-mindedness will seem natural, indeed essential because this is a 'hunting' environment. One or two women in this group will struggle with interaction, feeling uncared for or left out, and again criticised for not doing things right. So again, judgement and prejudice need to be replaced with understanding and loving action.

With regard to our personal relationships, each of us has surely suffered from this man brain/woman brain judgement trap many times. It leaves deep scars in most alcoholics.

Another angle on all this, and one that can be important for relationships within families, is how we raise children with the development of their own man brain or woman brain. We often use the expression 'roots and wings' in the Fellowship, where we learn about improving the upbringing that we give to our children and I believe that part of that is being properly supportive and constructive about all the elements of man-brain and woman-brain, and the associated instincts.

Social Stereotyping

I think a lot of modern social stereotyping problems come from a lack of understanding and respect for man-brain and woman-brain differences. Often these things are grossly distorted and even used as a driver for humour and other forms of entertainment

For example, there's a TV dating show in the UK where a large group of young women get introduced to a single man, then through a few short questions and some video clips of him, the women get to vote if they want to date him. One day some years ago this programme came on and the women in the room started discussing how, if it was the other way around (a large group of men choosing to go out with one girl), the men would purely vote on the woman's looks and take no account of her personality. The comments in the room became quite aggressive and I felt they were directed at me as a man. They were sneering that if a girl was 'a perfect ten' all the men would want to go out with her, and if a girl was anything much less than that, none of the men would date her. There were also comments that the programme was obviously made by men, that it was sexist and so-on. And of course, in the context of those people chosen for the programme, the objections were essentially true.

But this sort of bad thinking sticks. If we watch or hear enough of this stuff we become prejudiced by it. Another area of TV which particularly concerns me is the more aggressive soap operas where stereotyped behaviour between men and women is constant, as is the resultant destructive behaviour (including boozing) in the storylines.

We can't stop this stuff of course, any more than we can stop liquor companies making alcohol, but we can be clear in our own minds and our own relationships with people that these sorts of things should be avoided.

Same Sex Relationships

If we accept that man-brain and woman-brain exists, then what's the situation in same sex relationships? Are there any significant differences in relationships depending on physical sexual orientation? Yes there surely must be some but I think too much is made of our gender, sexual orientation and physical appearance based on prejudices regarding acceptability. What is significant is that humans are not the same. We have either a male or female body and either a male or female brain, and some are somewhere in between – that's how nature makes us (and God loves us).

So firstly, the notion that a relationship is 'same sex' could be a nonsense if one has a female brain and one a male brain. Or a couple could both have a 'neutral brain' so when it comes to hunting or cooking, they're about the same. And when it comes to attraction, then clearly those processes too can be on different parts of the scale.

Chapter Five – Working Recovery in a Relationship

I think I've made fairly good progress in my recovery – slowly crossing my personal bridge to normal living. In the early days, my recovery went in the usual way – accepting powerlessness, regaining some manageability, writing inventories and so-on, leading to better honesty, a sense of spirituality and the ability to put others before myself. After a while I was using all the recovery tools and they were having a good effect. I had also started my deeper work on the whole issue of relationships in recovery, and one pretty big question was starting to emerge; should there be any differences in the way we work our recovery if we're in a relationship compared to if we are single? I came to the conclusion that there should be.

Church Story

Let me go back in time, and tell you a story that became a significant catalyst for the start of my work on this book. In my early years of recovery I lived on my own in a small town in the heart of Wales. I moved there at the end of my marriage for the sustainment of my business. Luckily for me I already had about one year of recovery before making this move, because when I arrived I discovered there were no AA meetings within an hour's drive (in good weather). So I read what Bill W said about his early days and started to find other alcoholics in the town to start some meetings. It was hard going, and whilst I learned a lot, in the end I struggled because the few alcoholics I had found were so sick. I could not safely keep the meetings going, but I had to do something so I wondered if church could be a route to spiritual living for me.

At first I didn't feel inclined to do much religious worship – I'd never found church to my liking before. But one morning I awoke feeling pretty apprehensive about my situation, so I structured a clear thought in my mind and spoke it out loud. I said, "What should I do?" And the answer came back like a rocket – "go to church." And not any old church, but a specific church I had walked past many times in the town.

I went, and found they were great people. Spiritual, loving, caring and fun. It was a modern church and much to my surprise they were very aware of the problem of addiction, and ran an alcohol drop-in group on a Friday afternoon. I went to the group a few times but it was in the daytime and I was working, so I attended their house-groups in the evenings and found them excellent for my own wellbeing.

The people at this church spent most of their time being active in the local community and all around the world too. Some of those guys would sell their houses and use the money to go to Africa and dig toilets simply because that's what their higher power told them to do. I became close with the pastor and his family (we lived in the same street), and one day they explained that a big opportunity had come along; the chance to buy a much better church building. Now, in my professional life I had been well trained in putting together scientific papers, business cases and the like, and as this opportunity for the church was emerging, I had another clear message from my higher power – "Steve, you must help them put their business case together". It took a lot of time in my evenings, there were revenue streams, risk assessments and the like to work out. It succeeded; they got the mortgage a few months later.

Now, those gracious church folk were very grateful for my help, it had enabled them to fulfil their dreams of a much better church. But I learned something very important from all of this – having good humility and being right-sized doesn't mean you can't do big things. In AA, we have a very downward-pushing ego management approach because a big ego combined with our insanity can be a lethal combination, but equally we use the expression 'go to any lengths'. The attitude of religious folk is you absolutely must use all your skills to do God's will; they build things, create big ideas, run businesses in their churches, all stuff that we quite rightly don't do directly in AA.

But, where is the correct line between humility, going to any lengths and building big? I don't really know to be honest, but there are times when we have to be really constructive. Bill W got down to it and wrote the Big Book. But what I see now, is that one of the biggest things of all for each of us to build is a relationship, and a family. Most of those people in that church had made that one of their greatest tasks. Their love of God came first, but their personal relationships were definitely second.

Knowledge and Work

I now believe that recovering alcoholics who want to have a successful relationship need to have a better knowledge of the recovery process than someone who doesn't. That might sound unfair, I don't mean it to be, I just think it's true. And I say need, because whilst someone who is single may have the most fantastic knowledge of recovery possible, they probably don't need it as much as someone who's sharing a bed with another crazy human being.

Our wisdom has to be more developed to survive a relationship. I think we have to work our program in a different way, and apply our recovery principles in more depth. In fact, pretty much everything we learn in recovery, everything we discover about our character defects and everything we have to change, just has to be that bit deeper, that bit more intense and that bit more effective. But this is nothing new to anyone out there, living normal lives in normal relationships. The popular expression "you have to work at a relationship" is no different to our own "it works if you work it" mantra. Like recovery, if you're not prepared to work at a relationship, it will probably fail.

Getting Relationship Help in the Fellowship

If we have relationship problems, which in some ways means anyone in a relationship, then it's going to be vital to speak to people in the fellowship about it. I suggest you seek out people who have current experience with relationships themselves and seem to be reasonably successful in them. We soon get to know the wise-ones in our meetings, who are experts with the vast majority of recovery, but some of those may not be in tune with in-love relationship problems. I am not making assumptions here, I've asked many people and there are times when recovery gurus will agree they are not always best equipped to help out with relationship issues.

Maybe you can have a great sponsor for all the core stuff, for going through the steps, but you might find another good person to discuss relationships with. Be careful though, not to be too open about your relationship with lots of folks in the fellowship. I've seen people tell everyone about their relationship issues only later to see it lead to problems. You can attract the wrong sort of attention for a start, or get lots of conflicting feedback from people who don't really know the right thing for you. And whilst it's great to do open and honest shares in meetings, I have found it's best to keep some of the personal and intimate things just a little more private. You will find that usually in meetings people will mention the sex instinct briefly, just simple comments about it being something that can be out of balance. I think talking about sex in the same depth as discussed in the Big Book and the Twelve and Twelve is the maximum you should disclose in general shares. But on the other hand, make sure you don't end up burying relationship and sex instinct problems. You have to bring them out, but just with the right people.

Choosing a Good Sponsor

Here are the main points that I think are important when choosing a sponsor. Choose someone who you like and someone you feel comfortable talking too, who will give you enough of their time and who will be confidential. Choose someone who's recovery you respect and check your potential sponsor really has done the steps, and has a sponsor themselves. Find someone who has a good knowledge of the steps, the traditions, AA history and all the core literature of AA. Choose someone who is active in the fellowship on a broader level, a person who regularly chairs meetings, sponsors others, attends conventions etc. If you want to learn about the issues of having a relationship in recovery, then perhaps choose a sponsor who's in a good relationship. And highly preferably, someone of the same sex.

I do see problems when people choose sponsors. The primary one being picking someone who is talkative and easy-going because you want a person you can have a jolly good chat with, whereas you really should choose someone who you can have a bit of a chat with yes, but is going to get down to business too and maybe be firm with you when it's needed. Remember that the core reason for having a sponsor is to ensure you get honest about yourself and to lead you towards taking effective action about your character defects. You need someone who keeps focus on these objectives, and really goes through the work with you. And it can be quite tough at times – a sponsor needs to be quite analytical in order to understand his sponsee to the required depth, so that he or she can spot the self-deceiving processes that will be present in the sponsee's inventory and behaviour.

The sponsor needs to be a good teacher for sure, but you, the sponsee, need to be willing and teachable. It doesn't work if a sponsee has an attitude that he or she does't want to be told what to do. You have to find faith and trust in your sponsor to really work at the things they suggest. In my view it's only by working it this way that you start to get results.

I have recently started using the expression 'steps four, five, six and seven is the engine room of recovery'. You see, in steps one, two and three we talk about needing a power greater than ourselves – to me, that's the fuel. But all the drive is generated where that fuel is burnt, in the engine room. And then, once that energy is effectively harnessed, your ship-of-life gets underway, and you can start to put the harms done and wellbeing of others into good order again. But when you start, you don't know how to build a good engine room, you don't know how to take a good inventory or how to deal with those character defects that are ingrained into your personality. Your engine room won't ever propel your ship unless you get help building it. This is the primary job of the sponsor.

One thing of course, there is always a strong debate about opposite sex sponsoring and the risk that this might lead to inappropriate relationships. But risk management is always about balance of risk, and I have seen examples where other vitally important needs have been sensibly taken into account, and opposite sex sponsoring has worked well. For example, what if your AA meeting is in a quiet rural area with only a few members, when a newcomer turns up and no-one of the same sex is available to help them? Maybe it's only a person of the opposite sex who has the spare time, or lives near them. If you were potentially that person who could help, would you abandon the newcomer at the start of their recovery because they are the opposite sex? And sometimes people struggle badly in their recovery for a long time, have several sponsors over a few years, yet don't make any worthwhile progress. The horrors of relapse and depression seem unavoidable. Then finally they find someone who has the strength, determination, the right personal experiences and knowledge of the steps that just might be the key to unlocking their progress. If that were you, and you had reached such a point of pain, would you deny yourself the opportunity because the potential new sponsor was the opposite sex?

Measuring Success

Because we're attempting something pretty serious here, trying to understand all the extra work and responsibility required to have a successful relationship in sobriety, we have to dig quite a bit deeper into the recovery processes and develop them more.

But how do we know if we are doing what's required? There are many ways of defining the success criteria of recovery, achieving some peace of mind is one of my personal favourites. Using different ways of defining success in recovery is important – it helps us understand our own true level of knowledge and progress.

The most obvious measure, and the one we talk about the most, is our progress through the steps. We all know what the steps are, and I go through them in detail later with regards to focussing them on the needs of relationships. But I think there are two further useful measures, the first is what I call the five stages of acceptance.

The five stages of acceptance:

- Stage one is when the alcoholic has found AA but has not surrendered to their plight, and is still in and out of the rooms and drinking.
- Stage two is when the alcoholic accepts he/she is powerless over alcohol and that a higher power can restore sanity.
- Stage three is when the alcoholic accepts he/she needs to learn and properly work steps four, five, six and seven with a sponsor.
- Stage four is when the alcoholic accepts that he or she has to teach others and becomes a sponsor, taking their own sponsees through the steps.
- Stage five is when the alcoholic accepts that he or she has to apply the tools of recovery to all their affairs with the same level of diligence and responsibility that is required to beat alcohol.

Stage four is the first time we work with someone else's defects. This teaches us much more about the steps and how to be truly tolerant and loving towards someone else at depth. Stage four is also a vital springboard to stage five. As we sponsor someone else and help them to practice their principles in all their affairs, we see more clearly how we have to work hard to achieve the promises for ourselves – including a great relationship of course.

Here's something to try; think about the people you know in your meetings, how good their recoveries are and how settled and happy they seem to be in themselves, then look at which of these five levels they are at

– I think you will see a connection and be able to literally group people accordingly. It sounds a rather unpleasant judgmental thing to do, but really no more so than using the slogan "stick with the winners". The point is though, to reflect that back onto yourself and look at where you are with your own stages of acceptance.

Next is what I call the three phases of effectiveness. I came to see what might be a second rather uncomfortable truth about us all – some people were effective in their recoveries, and others were not, in a different way than whether they took a drink again, or went through the steps or did service. In essence, there are those that 'conceal', those that 'reveal' and those that 'deal' (with their defects).

The three phases of effectiveness:

Phase One – Conceal:

We all have masks we hide behind, and hiding is a process of concealment. We might hide behind our masks out of fear, and it may provide some form of safety in dangerous situations, with an abusive partner perhaps. But lots of concealing is part of the basic dishonesty problem and of course, the worst form of that is self concealing. I did that in my drinking days, I hid behind the mask of a good military man. It was only after I started going to AA that I slowly realised that I was nothing like the ideal guy I thought I was. In our bad drinking days we conceal so much of course, we use many masks to hide behind. And we can bring that into recovery – not writing down on our inventory what our real defects are, not discussing them with our sponsors, concealing our defects and pretending we are well. A lot of people do this and it's very unhealthy.

Phase Two – Reveal:

There are those people who constantly reveal. They talk all the time about their problems, to anyone who will listen. There's no sense and no progress from this sort of outpouring – we might think it's great to keep sharing but really we're probably just looking for sympathy in a rather selfish way. You might hear people say that their recovery is based on going to lots of meeting and sharing on their troubles, and how good that is for them. Or we can go to great efforts ourselves, pouring out our woes to caring sponsors – who probably listen for longer than they should. But if you think about that sort of behaviour, and watch it in others, you start to see that it's not really effective recovery either.

Phase Three – Deal:

So, looking a bit deeper again, we can then spot those that truly deal with their defects, take proper action according to the steps to replace undesirable defects with good principles. It's only these people that are finding the path to Bill's fourth dimensional living and having proper conscious contact with their higher power. And probably, it's only these types of recovering alcoholics who can have effective relationships.

Now please don't panic here, if you identify yourself more honestly as a concealer or revealer, remember, this is really just different words to describe the path of humility. But this description is useful for identifying if we're kidding ourselves or not – it's perhaps a practical measure of progress, a deep one admittedly, but if you can find the humility to be honest about where you are with this, then I think that's really important. And use the homesick tummy feeling as your guide. If you think you are concealing, how do you feel if you try and tell someone genuinely about a problem? If your stomach flips with a little fear then your emotions are probably trying to conceal. And as a result, do you generally tend to not open up much, keeping most of your feelings locked away? The same then goes if you can tell people about your faults, can talk about it a lot and quite easily, but then have that sick feeling when occasionally someone pushes back against you a little and says something like "well, why don't you actually take some action about this problem?" If that makes your stomach flip, then perhaps you are at the reveal stage. If however, you've managed to change that to a sort of contented, warm feeling when someone genuinely points out a character defect and how you might deal with it, then wow. That's a great thing that shows huge amounts of humility and acceptance, and a genuine spiritual awakening to the actual processes of recovery.

To me, a big part of the end-game is getting to that point where someone can tell you you're wrong, and your automatic reply is "okay, what do you think I should do about it?" And without the sick stomach feeling.

Read a Lot of Literature

One thing that I often see in the fellowship is this; people who read a lot of books about recovery, old or new, approved literature or not, seem to have a better recovery than those who don't. It's strange, some people seem to insist on only reading and working from the Big Book. Bill W never said to do this. I think that if someone is stubbornly sticking to only the Big Book, it's a reflection of the fear and lack of willingness that still remains unresolved in that individual.

Certainly in my view, the Twelve and Twelve is vital studying after the big book, as it contains essential amplification of the steps. That's why they wrote it. All the rest of Bill W's writing, Grapevine and Share magazine and books from good publishers like Hazelden are great too. Good speaker tapes (or the apps for them) are also a good way to expand our knowledge. I think that everyone writes or speaks from a different experience and a unique relationship with their higher power, and this always reveals something new to the reader. This is, in a way, part of the social instinct whereby we always learn from contact with others, even in writing. We get some new insight into recovery or spirituality, and we can use that to better develop our own sobriety.

I have, on many occasions, thought I've known about myself in a particular regard, gone on for years maybe, thinking I have dealt with something effectively, then suddenly I hear or read something pertinent to me that puts a new vital piece of information into my head. I now know something (about myself) I didn't know before. And we must keep practicing the process of letting outside guidance in.

We all have choice in what we study, and fundamentally it's up to each of us what we work with. But I believe that here, if we are thinking about embarking on a successful relationship and taking responsibility for it, then more study has to be better. And hey, you could even do your studies together – my wife and I do.

Complexity Theory

Many years ago I attended a course in the USA on complexity theory. This is a pretty dull but essential subject in certain fields – and it's mostly maths. It was developed as a set of tools to identify and quantify the increasing risk management burden in big organisations such as banks that are using more and more complex information and communication systems all the time. At the strategic level it talks about how, when any situation becomes more complex (more factors and variables), more effort is required to keep things in control. And also that when things go wrong in a more complex system, the consequences can be more severe.

I think complexity theory is useful to keep in mind when we are examining our lives and our recovery. Highlighting, if you like, that we all have varying amounts of complexity to deal with. Consider the people you know well in the fellowship, some may be long into recovery and single, with no immediate family ties and are financially stable enough to have little to worry about. Whereas others, even with a good few years under their belts, still have tough working lives, big families, lots of bills to pay and so-on. Add to that a relationship, and you're certainly going to see more complexity for those people.

I think this is why in meetings you sometimes find some people saying very strongly "keep it simple", because keeping it simple works for them – their lives are genuinely quite simple. But those with significant complexity can't find any real solution that way, at first at least. I think you can distill some things down to simple concepts, and we certainly want to avoid the turmoil that leads to stress and depression, but it's inevitable I think that we are going to require different levels of recovery effort, not only because our inner faults might be different, but also because our lives have different levels of complexity.

I've had to use the steps with greater vigour than other people in certain areas in order to deal with specific problems in my life. My personal relationships have been one driver, but another example is that I'm a businessman, and that throws up lots of problems with manageability, acceptance, ego and so-on. Accepting a customer yelling down the phone at you, and having to do something quickly about it, feels different from more normal types of pressure you have to face, such as the acceptance you have for the lovely but quirky people you see in meetings. A few years ago my pride was hurt rather publicly when a product I had designed had some bad-press in a trade journal and this feels quite different to the hurt you might feel remembering your past drinking escapades. In the end though, they are not really different, all I'm saying is, if your life is more complex you're likely going to get hit with more potentially hurtful challenges.

And this immediately brings up the next big question. Is such extra complexity worth it? Should I go through all of the problem-solving processes about my complex issues, dealing with them using the spiritual toolset, or should I stop them completely – dump it all, in essence? But how to decide? Well, it's all down to what type of rewards you want to get out of life I think. Although we're not special and different in terms of our alcoholism, we are quite different in some of our other life situations. As I've said, some people want the simple life, other's want, or have, lots more complexity. This takes us to gratitude, which is where the answer to this dilemma lies I think. Are you truly grateful that you're in a relationship, or hold a busy job? Do the positives outweigh the negatives? Is the spiritual effort you have to put in more than equalled by the spiritual wellbeing you're getting out of it? By the way, I don't recommend you rush into decisions in these areas in early recovery. It's not easy I found, to determine the pro's and cons. This is something that should be worked-through in depth with your sponsor. You need analysis and guidance for sure but also you need to build your own experience and understanding of complex issues – I think it's a fundamental keystone in your bridge to normal living.

And... Keeping it Simple

In the paragraphs above I mentioned 'keeping it simple'. This slogan is used all the time in the Fellowship, but honestly, I think it confuses a lot of people. A sponsee of mine once said "I don't find the literature simple at all, the Twelve and Twelve seems very complicated to me and I struggle to take it in when I read it – even words like pride and humility have so many different meanings".

Complexity theory as I discussed earlier, also covers complex equipment or machines. And again I've had a lot of experience in this area – I once worked extensively with maintenance and flight operations of aircraft, and worked on some new aircraft development projects too. So let me build a 'keep-it-simple' analogy using a large aircraft as the example.

When an aircraft is first designed and the first one or two are built as flight-test aircraft, the whole process is a complicated thing. Thousands of design drawings, hundreds of equipment suppliers, assembly in a giant hangar, testing, measurements, re-design when it's not quite right and so-on. Then flight testing in all weathers to analyse all the pilot's handling considerations and how the aircraft flies with systems out or an engine down.

Then all this complex work has to be distilled down. Is it going to be safe and easy in normal service for a pilot to know what's going wrong when he has a failure? Do the systems give him the right alarm indications or can the system automatically start-up a duplicate? Do the pilot's notes give him exactly the right information in the easiest possible format? And how is essential maintenance done safely after a flight and the aircraft refuelled and checked ready to go again?

'Designing-in' the keeping-it-simple is the answer – like this. If the pilot has some problems before a flight, a couple of little systems playing up say, he'll report it to the ground engineers. The engineers will go to a few test panels in the belly of the aircraft, push a couple of 'press-to-test' buttons and see what results they get, usually a fault code. They find that code in a manual that tells them where the problem probably is and which component to change. Most components in the electronic systems in an aircraft are modular, they are in a metal case with plugs on the back. All the engineer does is slide out the one that is faulty and slide in a new one. He then goes back to the test panel and pushes the 'press to test' button again. If it passes the test this time, his work is done and he finishes by signing the paperwork.

Indeed, for every possible fault on an aircraft there is either an automatic test, or a manual test using additional test equipment that the ground engineers have available. And to support this, what the engineers actually have is an office (or an iPad) full of maintenance manuals that cater for every scenario. And if the fault is too bad to fix quickly at the aircraft ramp, the manuals say that too. Something like "This fault requires the replacement of hydraulic pump number four. This work will take approx 8 hours to complete". The engineer tells the captain, the captain tells the passengers and everyone gets out the plane. Funny though, how we all moan and cuss at this point, but would you rather the engineers didn't have all those test schedules available and your plane took off with a failing hydraulic pump?

That office full of maintenance manuals is how they keep it simple – in the moment. The aircraft is not simple. But any and every action that is required is written down step-by-step, easy to follow and gets a desired result – the plane works again. I see this as an analogy to our broken spiritual condition and the tools of recovery. The work that went into creating the twelve steps and its supporting literature, and the creation of the fellowship and all its administration is actually pretty complex (try attending a few intergroup or region meetings). The standard recovery tools allow us to apply the operational and maintenance tasks required in a relatively simple way for early recovery and general living. I am suggesting that when undertaking a serious relationship, there's going to be a requirement for additional manuals. And by the way, if the destination is not worth going too, then re-plan and divert the flight – go somewhere that's going to be lovely, with a bit of sunlight to relax in.

Some Useful Things from My Own Change Processes

In my early years of recovery I went through the steps as best I could, listening and learning. Then with my first inventory I tried to list my grosser character defects and went through them with another human being. I didn't really get the 'sharing with a higher power' thing very much at that time. And later, as I got to step ten, I tried to recognise my defects as they materialised, rather than listing problems from my memory of the past.

At first I would reflect back at the end of some of my days, usually the tougher days, when things had gone wrong. I also started to genuinely investigate the idea of spiritual living by doing more service in the fellowship and reading more AA literature. It was a year or two later that I started to consider the principle of contempt prior to investigation when it came to God, noting that people who spoke out strongly in favour of a higher power seemed happier in themselves.

There are two items in the spiritual toolkit that I really like – the Just for Today card and the Serenity Prayer. I was using the serenity prayer whenever I was getting hurt, frustrated (when I could not control a situation) or had messed up again (and felt pain or guilt). But in those early days I'd use the serenity prayer after the event. For example, I would use it to recover from the pain after someone hurt me – until I was told to use the prayer before I was hurt. You see, if someone is going to hurt me usually know that it's coming. We are hurt by uncaring or vexatious people so why would it be a surprise when they do hurt us again? You've probably tried to change them before, letting them know that they keep hurting you, but they won't change. So we should be wise to that risk by now. And we know that if they do say something hurtful, its our over-sensitive nature or self pity that is going to generate that hurt, so again we know beforehand where the pain is really going to come from – our own character defects. So we accept that we can't change the other person, before the event, and accept our potential part in it (being hurt if they say something), again before the event. What I have had the courage to change is how prepared I am – the nasty comment is going to come and I know it's going to come, and I'm prepared. And I am ready with the reaction of the good principle, not the reaction of my defect. I quickly deflect the pain and bring in my acceptance and my contact with my higher power.

And I found if I regularly used the serenity prayer before an upset, I did get wiser. I became more effective at predicting when something was likely to cause me stress, or even better, avoiding the stressful event altogether. It's actually worth seriously looking at this particular aspect – can you actively and effectively head it off at the pass? I don't mean by rudely avoiding people or not dealing with things that need to be confronted, but do you play your part in keeping yourself out of the firing line?

Another thing with the serenity prayer, you'll have noticed the way it is usually printed, with four of the key words enlarged for emphasis. Well, I have started reading just the large words, from bottom to top, WISDOM > COURAGE > SERENITY > GOD. I later discovered this is not new (nothing ever is) but the benefit of doing this had passed me by for quite a while. Next time you're sat round the table in a meeting, just listening, try reading the big words in reverse order a few times – I'm sure you'll get it.

The Just for Today card is great at settling me down, and reminding me to make allowances in the day, to put other people first, but also to make some me-time. And there are some very clever clues in there about the basic but troublesome problems we have in relationships. Next time you read the Just For Today card, think about it in terms of how well you do all those things with your partner, and then think about your overall humility. You see, I think it takes much more humility and deeper sacrifice to do those things constantly and effectively with a partner than it does say three times a week at your meetings. One thing I have found with the just for today card is to change two words of the last sentence so it becomes 'to believe that as I give to my partner, so my partner will give to me'. This is one of the the greatest practical changes you can make for a successful relationship.

But what about my main change processes? Well they're based around steps six and seven of course, but the lightbulb moment for me there was hearing Joe and Charlie's version of the replacement process. You can't just try and remove a defect on its own, it leaves a hole. You have to replace it with the opposite, or God's will, or love, or the right thing, and so-on. Joe and Charlie's idea of a business and bad stock-in-trade is perfect. If I don't throw out the bad stock and replace it with good, my business is going to go bankrupt for sure. This idea is what then led me to work through my own inventory at depth, and I slowly formed all my own principles to practice.

Then as I practice my step ten processes more, I get better at it, but sometimes I still find faults. Here's an example of one that happened recently. It was a Saturday and my wife had planned to go to a lunchtime meeting some distance away, on her own (as we sometimes do of course). She was going to meet one of her sponsees there, but also a newcomer. Kathryn said she would aim to get back fairly promptly, so we could do something together later in the day. That sounds good I thought, I'll do some business in the morning, then go to the gym for a nice workout at lunchtime. Well, I was bounced with an unplanned Skype call and didn't get to the gym until later (so starting to feel a little grumpy already). Then

I didn't get a text from Kathryn around the time I was expecting, to say she was on her way back home. I carried on in the gym for longer, then went and had a long swim and a soak in a jacuzzi. Now I'm sure you all know that feeling – my day had been pushed out of kilter, and now I'm projecting that Kathryn has forgotten about our plans for later, and having a lovely time in a cafe chatting to all her female recovery buddies. After a while I started to change my thinking. "I'm here now with this micro resentment, and it's almost certainly not based in the truth, so just accept it." But I still felt just a little bit bad, but about myself now, and boom, there it is, that's the real wrong for my step ten, in fact there is a stack of wrongs if you break it down. I'm being wrong in my thinking and need to promptly admit and do something better about it than this. So then I thought, I'm the luckies man alive with the most beautiful wife, and she's driven 45 minutes each way to do work with other alcoholics. And (forcing the replacement process), I'm here sober, enjoying the fruits of my work in a fancy gym. But then I get to the even more important bit (another stack), Kathryn knows she's running late and is probably slightly worrying about that, and if I, just the tiniest bit, express that I'm upset that she's late, then that really is the wrong thing to do. Smiling to myself and pondering this even more, I convert the feelings into that area of freedom and joy that we're both doing the will of our higher power. When she calls a while later she immediately apologises for being late, I reply saying that considering she was meeting two alcoholics who needed her help, no wonder her timings overran. Kathryn then said she was relieved that I was okay about it all. Tea and medals for me? Not really, I should have short-cut straight to the right attitude from the start.

Inventory Cycles and Change

There are many ways that people go about their recovery. I'm sure it varies greatly depending on what type of person you are, what your circumstances are, what you like and dislike in the recovery toolset and what your sponsor thinks. And there are probably regional and country differences too. Some people stick more to the Big Book, other's get more from the Twelve and Twelve, or 'Joe and Charlie' (see References).

Whatever route you take, surely the goals are the same – a daily reprieve from alcohol – with lots of spiritual wellbeing and a productive and enjoyable life. But to achieve those goals there are two core things that I think have to happen – taking inventory and making change. Fact finding, fact facing and replacing bad stock with good is another way of putting it. And as I said earlier, this comes from steps 4-7, the engine-room steps.

There are different ways we can take inventory and create change and I'd like to suggest some processes here that have worked well for me. And I think they can lead to a much more effective style of joint recovery for people in relationships. But I want to be really clear here – the following inventory/change cycles are just my own ideas. I hope they are of value for you to discuss and consider but please form your own opinion and make your own judgement on their value or suitability for you.

The Early Recovery Cycle

When we first come into the rooms we must focus all our effort on not picking up a drink, getting familiar with the fellowship and making new friends. After a while we should think about getting a sponsor. Your new sponsor should start by taking you through steps 1-3, then get you moving forward on the inventory and change work. The first few times that you look at the information on your inventory, and start making change, is what I call the early recovery cycle.

The Early Recovery Cycle goes like this:

- We start to build an inventory of the past. Not a life story, but inventory items selected correctly in accordance with the Big Book. Resentments, harms, fears and sex conduct. And we make sure that we start to identify our part in the items on the list.
- We start to share this information with God and another human being (our sponsor at this time). And we need to start some analysis here, working with our sponsor to really seek out and face the truth about our own behaviour. We must identify our own character defects, and not the defects of the other people on the list – an important start to the work required for a good relationship of course.
- Then we look more closely at our grosser handicaps, remembering it takes courage to face them. Our sponsor helps us start the analysis process. Perhaps initially we don't do anything much to try and change our faults – at this stage we just have to get used to facing our shortcomings as we will likely be fearful or ashamed of what we find. And this is where the first real, and probably the most important experience of acceptance starts (no good trying to accept that you're powerless over alcohol, but not accepting the real defects that cause your alcoholism). Acceptance of ourselves with clarity and without denial is essential. Also at this stage we start making simple amends to people close to us – not formally apologising, just reducing our selfish behaviour is the amends we're after.

- Then we try to change some of these defects. I found that the St Francis prayer was a great way for me to understand that the way to remove defects was to identify them; "where there was ..." and replace them "let there be ..." As I identified each defect, I realised that the defect felt like an obsession in my head, when active it filled my thinking and I never thought of much else. Yet when I fought it and though about goodness, kindness and love instead, I felt an easing of the insanity in my mind. I had a sense of comfort, only fleetingly at first, that I had done something good. Here was a hint of spirituality.
- In parallel with this, we start to identify with the new friends that we find in the fellowship. But we should be careful here not to try and match our early chaos with some of the other new folks in the meeting who might also be struggling, but instead we should try and connect our growing serenity with those people we can see have genuinely good recovery.
- And remember, because it is a cycle, you don't get everything fixed on the first, second or fifth time round. You make some progress then go back around again. I often used to lose the comforting feeling that I had done something good, it would get replaced again by the bad behaviour or bad feelings, until I remembered (or was told) to do the right thing again and again. It's practice.
- The role of your sponsor in all this is to keep you honest, but also to pace you, going too slow, or too fast is to be avoided, and that varies for everyone.

There is another way that I sometimes look at the early recovery cycle. Imagine a horizontal line that represents the results of your early recovery. The left hand part of the line is living in insanity, with the first drink at the very end. Looking along the line to the right we get to the part that is living in the early solution, which is somewhere around the middle of the line. Moving from the left hand end to the middle represents that initial, early progress through the steps. The right hand end of the line represents our first sense of serenity and an awareness that the promises might be real.

So I call this line the early recovery spectrum. We start at the left when we first come into the rooms. We work to defeat the drink and reduce unmanageability, aiming to get our step work underway and start getting some positive results. Now I think getting positive results is critical here, particularly a little bit of peace and serenity. In a way, this is the antidote to white knuckling it or being a dry drunk. It's not really about getting off the booze, but getting some good results to replace the booze. Our brain only knows one way out of the pain of our character defects so far, and that's drinking, and our brain will only lock onto something else if that makes us feel good too. So we have to learn to feel good with something better than drink.

And this phase is, I suppose, how most people think recovery goes on, forever. But I don't – it's in the next recovery cycle where things really start to progress.

The Established Recovery Cycle

This cycle has some similarities to the early recovery cycle, but also some very important differences about change.

The Established Recovery Cycle goes like this:

- Fundamentally, our inventory now becomes an inventory of the present. We are looking for things that are now causing us pain or unmanageability in our sober day, not in our drinking past (although they can stem from the past). These issues tend to be lower-level, less obvious disturbances within our spiritual selves, maybe caused by continued fear or anxiety, or perhaps practical issues such as unhappiness with a job or a relationship. However, these things can still significantly disrupt our present and future lives.

- So again we share these problems with our sponsor and higher power, looking for the truth, but this time in creative and constructive ways to resolve the more difficult issues that we see. Can we use more acceptance or is our current life situation not working for us? Is what we are doing with our lives really God's will for us? Have we found the right solutions or do we need to do deeper study into the Twelve and Twelve say?

- And then we should be identifying areas in our lives that need to change. But I now think of this more as situations to change and experience to be gained rather than defects to be removed.

- If we don't start practicing this established recovery cycle then we are storing-up long term problems in my view. For example, we might feel trapped, our destiny feels wrong or we can't remove recurring resentments.

When we view the established recovery cycle in terms of a results spectrum, it has changed now. The left hand portion of the line becomes living in dishonesty. That is, knowing (even subconsciously) that you are not on the path of destiny, humility and service that you should be on. And at the far left hand end of the line now lies depression. If you stay in this zone, without implementing the necessary change that is required for your long-term wellbeing, you cannot function properly using God's will – blocked-off from the sunlight of the spirit, as Bill called it. Stay there even longer and that depression might just suddenly snap you back to a drinking binge as your brain fights for the only thing it can remember makes it happy.

The right hand part of the line is therefore living in serenity, honesty and joy – knowing that you are on the humility path that you should be on. The very right hand end of the line represents, if you like, the perfect grace and humility that only God can have.

The established recovery cycle is so important in my view. It introduces a new way of looking at where we are and where we're going and includes the idea of where depression might come from. And it also brings in the concept of planning. If, with your sponsor you can see what still needs changing (planning), then these things become the next items to change. Some of these things may seem overly difficult, and people hide them away as what you might call hidden fears. But if they are there, they will certainly stop you from finding the things you want in life.

The Relationship Recovery Cycle

This is a combination of both the early and established recovery cycles – it needs to combine both because, within a relationship, you will have to look at more things from the past again as well as the present. It took me a while to grasp this important point myself and I think it's required because with a relationship you are building something new and the defects from your individual pasts will have new and different effects as a couple. And you're also going to get big changes in your instincts – how your instincts feel and react will become very different. So you work this inventory with your partner, although you will probably involve your sponsors too, as new things are revealed to you both.

WORKING RECOVERY IN A RELATIONSHIP

The Relationship Recovery Cycle goes like this:

- We start by reviewing our character defects from both the past and the present, looking for those items that might cause unmanageability or fear for the other partner, or need improving to make our relationship a happier one. Don't underestimate this activity – this is a big thing, and a pretty tough yet fundamentally important concept. I think most of us would instinctively know that this is required as soon as we start to properly love a partner. You will sense the effects that your own defects have on the other person, finding it objectionable that your defect is causing the other person pain, fear or worry. And some defects may not be apparent to you – your partner may tell you about them first.

- We inventory our instincts in more depth. As we have been discussing, a relationship has significantly more power over our instincts than we might realise, so we need to increase the work here too. But we should be positive about it – this is more a journey of exploration than fault finding.

- And we need to inventory unmanageability. Honestly, I have seen so many relationships start well, where the romance and sex starts out strongly, only to see one or both people crumble later under the mounting complexity of it all.

- Doing the relationship recovery cycle well demands further development in trust and humility. And an even stronger mental attitude towards constructive progress, including the openness to avoid things going unsaid or unresolved. And progress will be limited if one person is not as committed to this process as much as the other. People always say a relationship requires trust and work, but how many people really do it to this level?

- You should also occasionally stand back and look again to see if you're both in the relationship for the right reasons. Is it an honest relationship and is it remaining honest? Are you both spiritually well within the relationship? You need to look at your plans and be prepared to change things if they are not right. You must both avoid feeling trapped or that your future together feels wrong. I suppose, in summary, if an established relationship is not honest and comfortable and you don't have a deep love for each other, it's going to take one or both of you towards either depression or a drink. You simply can't expect to have a long-term happy relationship under the wrong conditions.

It can be a bit of a shock at the beginning of a relationship, finding that you have some hitherto undetected defects. You will find things that just didn't materialise before, or things that you were aware of but their significance has now changed. You have to accept that this is going to happen because a new relationship (or improving an old relationship) pushes you into new territory, just the same as a new job might do. You will have to examine things and change things that would not be necessary if you were single.

If you look at couples in bad relationships, they struggle to agree on things and frequently argue – then feel resentment because they can't make productive changes or accept their differences. This deadlock has to be broken, else it turns into a corrosive thread of fear. And here, resentment is the type where the replay machine runs and runs behind the scenes, and it can take the form of blaming ourselves rather than the other person. We then become exhausted as we desperately try and incorrectly manage the imbalances of both ourselves and our partner.

At this point I think it might be useful to give an example of two clashing faults between myself and Kathryn. One is instinctive and one is learned. I thought I understood my instinct driven mechanisms of jealousy, and thought I could control its effect, but in the early days of my relationship with Kathryn, jealousy crept in a little when Kathryn went to her own meetings, or dinners with work colleagues. I would never try and stop her, or complain, but somehow I would give myself away, just a little, that I was uncomfortable. And Kathryn had suffered an unhappy relationship where a previous partner significantly controlled her activities based on his jealousy, so of course any form of jealousy on my part was triggering an enhanced (learned) defence mechanism in her. So, my natural instinct verses my desire not to behave with jealousy were in conflict, and Kathryn was hitting an over-sensitive defence mechanism about lack of freedom in relationships, and neither of us liked the uncomfortable feelings these things were creating.

So we worked on it, but couldn't completely eliminate these feelings either. What we slowly found was this – what remains from the jealousy problem is a little bit of jealousy-based fear, driven by instinct, and what remains of the fear of control is a slight oversensitivity to it, driven by bad past experience. But we can quantify it now, see it, control it.

What's funny is the real fear that there's always a small possibility that each could lose the other through some terrible accident or illness. We add grace and humility to the mix and share and laugh about those past faults now – realising we are both flawed but love each other anyway.

But here's an interesting thing. The idea of replacing character defects with the opposites, gaining the qualities of good honesty and good humility, using courage and strength to allow that process, and so-on, develops even further when you're in a relationship. Just think about it, with your sponsor you can always get away with not being completely honest, and you report back to them anecdotally that you are making improvements,. But with a partner they experience first hand how you are, and they see directly if you are making improvements or not.

The Steps Overlay For Relationships

It's essential of course, that every recovering alcoholic carries on with their step work all the way through their life, no matter what their circumstances. But for me, a big question started to emerge – would it be beneficial to change any emphasis or process in our step work that would help us in a relationship? And could that be done safely without risking any other essential aspects of recovery? I came to the conclusion that you could, and I called it the steps overlay.

What I'm suggesting here is that we overlay additional processes onto our 12 step work, enhance them if you like, specifically for the issue of in-love and relationships. I realised that the steps of AA are focussed on one person, they have to be – our 'selves' are unmanageable. But if there is more than one self closely involved, as there is in a relationship, perhaps we can develop some valuable additional points for the steps. The only area that I haven't detailed any specific change here is steps eight and nine. The process of making amends to other's we have harmed doesn't need to change and the process of making amends to our partners when required is really described within the core elements of the rest of the book.

Step One

If you're in a relationship as an active alcoholic, and are starting recovery, there can be an immediate and unexpected problem – as you start to comprehend the gravity of your situation you also become aware of your partners true situation. If you have progressed down the usual alcoholic path, causing all that destruction and pain to everyone around you, you're going to see the damage you have done and experience your partner's bad feelings towards you.

Feelings always flood in as you put down the booze. But in a personal relationship you have even deeper feelings buried in there, waiting to come out. Add that your partner is deeply hurt too and you can see the scale of the problem.

Step one is about admitting we are powerless: over alcohol (permanently) and manageability (temporarily). And it's here that we first see that drinking has been our only solution for when we can't cope. We try and stay off the booze one day at a time but we're in a state of shock too, so how those people around us do or don't support us can be critical. We can't expect them to get all enthusiastic about the Big Book, or God – it's natural that they're going to be pretty cynical at the start. But sometimes the damage can be so bad that a partner is like a cornered animal that's wounded and fighting for survival. This is a great risk to early recovery.

When a relationship has broken down so badly it's usually abusive and aggressive, and might cause so much daily pain that we have no chance of staying away from a drink. So, as it says in the AlAnon step one, we also need to learn how we are powerless over other people who are badly damaged. We can't afford, in early recovery, to miss this critical point. We may or may not try and fix our partner – certainly trying to fix (trying to have power over) a partner is not going to work, but just being in the line of fire, suffering the retribution, might be too much for us.

Now please don't get me wrong here, I'm not saying you must not consider your responsibilities, not to love or not to care... do those things if you can. But we have to be real – at this time you are mortally wounded too – you might have to get safe and live to fight another day.

Another big aspect around step one is that people who don't understand alcoholism never quite get that we really are totally powerless over it. If we're starting to get sober with a partner or family who are normal drinkers, don't be surprised if they start putting pressure on you to drink again. It probably won't be direct pressure, but the social position of drinking is a strange thing among people who can't get their head around the prospect of you and them being happy and functional without you doing some drinking. "Surely you can have a glass of wine with Christmas dinner – everyone's gone to such an effort"?

Perhaps I should share that some years into my recovery I started a relationship with someone who was a normal drinker. At first it seemed okay, and occasionally I did get the Christmas wine pushed my way (which I turned down of course), but over a longer period of time it became a big problem. My partner's drinking slowly increased and when she went out on her own with friends she would occasionally get falling-over drunk. I'd have to collect her from town (and her drunk friends), and clean up the mess. I tried for quite some time to be okay with this but in the end I just couldn't. I don't think her friends resented that I didn't drink, but they seemed extra determined to make sure my partner got hammered when I wasn't there. I also knew that there was a lot of drunken flirting going on with some of the other people who would be out. So you can see, the reminders of heavy drinking and the doubts about behaviour on boozy nights was just too unsettling for me. I kept being pulled back to living in the problem, even though it wasn't me doing the drinking.

Steps Two and Three

In recovery, we come back to the concepts of steps two and three all the time. When we first hear what these steps are though, we tend to rebel. The first obstacle is God of course, as to go from reckless boozer to bible-basher just seems ridiculous – and it's the easiest thing to throw such an idea out on its arse. But in a way that's the point. Can you find enough trust in the founders of AA to genuinely go along with the need for a higher power?

The big book gives you all the history, the stories and the reasons why. The Doctor's Opinion says how alcoholics are in essence lost causes until they experience a spiritual awakening. If you're not up to speed with all this then please take a refresher – it's important.

I think in essence steps two and three deal with insanity – the idea that we are not equipped to run the show. So we need something better than ourselves to guide our lives, we simply cannot make good decisions and take good action ourselves, and to think we can is insane (based on all the evidence).

Let's look at this now with two relationship scenarios. The first is a relationship where one or both are just into recovery, maybe even with a few relapses thrown in. The insanity here can be very high with rapid swings between huge resentments and fights, and a co-dependency process of seeking guidance and approval from the other partner. The point is that as well as the alcoholic's insanity, the relationship is effectively insane too. By the same measures, the track record of the relationship is poor, most of the decision and action taking mechanisms within the relationship are broken and the conclusion must be that the relationship needs something better than itself to guide it.

At the other end of the scale, take a relationship where both people are in long-term recovery and the relationship is functional and happy. By this time they have almost certainly worked out an effective mechanism to encompass steps two and three. First they will have been through the steps at great depth for themselves (with their own sponsors), and therefore will have mapped out how each thinks as an individual, and will have developed good handing-over and not-controlling processes. Then they will also have worked out a way of being effectively supportive and dependent on each other. Not overly dependent, but like anything in normal living – dependent to the right level. Kind and fair discussion and decisions about what each wants and needs, and taking joint responsibility to bring a feeling of freedom (from crazy thinking), trust and genuine love.

Steps Four and Five

Hopefully we all understand the critical importance of taking inventory and the need to share that inventory with God and another human being. We have to identify our character defects correctly. Correctly stems from the need to be honest, and we check the correctness by sharing them with other people who have the experience to understand them. Now, if you and your parter feel you are both ready, you can share them with each other. Easy to say but maybe not so easy to do at first (I have presumed of course you've already done some inventories with a sponsor). We are naturally more fearful of sharing our deepest faults with a partner than a sponsor.

And none of us wants to be in a relationship with someone who gets angry all the time, or who is riddled with fear. If defects like that are coming out in the relationship then you simply must try and take ownership of them and tell your partner you know your faults. If you deny them in the heat of the moment, they are going to start building additional resentments and fears. So I can't see any feasible way forward other than to inventory them between you. From my experience in my relationship now, once we got over the worry of truly admitting to each other our defects, we actually discovered more about them, found more of the root causes if you like (especially about traumatic issues from previous relationships), followed by many joyous lightbulb moments as we finally discovered deeper truths about ourselves.

When Kathryn and I decided to get married, with a full church wedding, it was actually as a result of this inventorying process that we felt ready. It cemented our understanding of such a commitment and it all connected with the proposition of the wedding vows (the vows took on huge context and value). Just think, how many people get married and glibly say the vows without any robust structure to underpin them? Also, because we had both found a spiritual faith with our higher powers, and feel as though we have been deliberately brought together, the full wedding service was a tremendous spiritual affirmation of everything we try to be for each other, and for God.

Coming back to the inventory process as a couple, I think it also does great things for humility and trust. The humility to work on deep defects with each other and deal with them without defensive or aggressive reactions. And with the trust that the other person won't judge you for them. Building this process means you reduce the fear of messing up a little bit now and then too. We're far from perfect and our defects are going to pop up from time to time.

Steps Six, Seven, Ten and Eleven

I've grouped six, seven, ten and eleven together because they all relate to change. Steps six and seven teach us how to go about change, and step ten tells us how we must apply those lessons on a daily basis – with everything. But I think it's actually step eleven that's the driver for change when we're in long-term recovery, and a relationship.

To see how this might be, let's work in reverse: step eleven, step ten, step seven and then step six, in a relationship context. As a relationship builds we become aware of the increasing emotional bond and spiritual closeness between us. And we want things to go well day-by-day, so naturally we think along the lines of step ten. Sometimes our thoughts are quite simple, like we don't want to do something that might upset the other person. But it should build to be more positive than that – we want the other person to feel confident and secure everyday (emotional security), and to just enjoy the relationship. And in that respect, you could say the joy is to feel confident in the love between you.

And it's here that I think we find step eleven, and why in a way it comes first. Conscious contact with our higher power and knowledge of his will for us – haven't we learned by now that fundamentally his will for us is to love others? He showed us at the start of our recovery that we needed others to love us – those people who worked with us, supported us and had endless patience to help us. To me, conscious contact is that practical love flowing into us – sometimes fatherly, sometimes like a good wing-man and sometimes even, with good humour. And in our early days when we kept messing up, didn't those good fellowship people just pick us up again? They were doing their higher power's will of loving us, every day. So it's the ideal of step eleven, delivered daily through step ten. And when a partner comes along it's no different – His will is that you love them properly too.

The step ten 'when I am wrong, promptly admit it' process changes through your recovery. It matures when you start to do service. An example might be you start to help your first newcomer and realise it's going to be quite an effort. You might think you can't be bothered with this difficult person but immediately you can feel how that thought is so wrong, promptly admit it to yourself, and so you carry on with your newcomer. Your higher-power's love, through you, drives the action. And carrying out this particular action is possibly the first properly responsible thing that we ever do for someone else.

WORKING RECOVERY IN A RELATIONSHIP

There's always a lot of stuff happening in a relationship and it's here that step ten has to grow and become strong. The sheer position of being wrong is such a stumbling block for some people, but you simply have to admit you're wrong, quickly and with humility and grace. But immediately, the other person has to accept it with even more humility and grace. Let's flip that around and think about it more – it's a critical point. If your partner does something wrong they're going to feel a bit upset or stupid or something (assuming it's nothing serious), and they're going to have to dig out a bit of humility to admit to it. But if you don't instantly receive their admission with even more care, ensuring you don't react with anger or ridicule say, you might do more damage than the original mistake. Two wrongs don't make a right, and this is a case where the second wrong is far worse than the first. If left unchecked, this lack of empathy in the moment leads to fear and a lack of honesty.

So rather than being wrong becoming a problem between you, embrace it, love it. But of course, dealing with things straight away can get a little tricky at times. You have to work at the balance of being ready to admit a mistake promptly yet not instantly throwing your hands up in dismay and begging for mercy. Or equally, not instantly jumping on a mistake by your partner without kindness and thought (this could fall into the category of reckless truth-telling). So sometimes you need to find the right time to raise things and only raise them if it's correct to do so. When it comes to mentioning someone else's defect, my wife often shares how she has linked the think – think – think card with the saying "is it the truth, is it necessary to say it and is it the kind and loving thing to do?" She uses these tools to check herself in the heat of the moment.

But of course there's more to all this yet. An opposite trap if you like, is to keep making mistakes and to keep promptly admitting them without constructive action for improvement. This now brings us back to steps six and seven – removing a defect by humbly asking God. So there's the humility word again but this time not directed towards your partner, but to God. Very clever this – can you see how it focusses on the relationship between you and God as the process for your mistakes and defects? Crying for forgiveness from a partner gets incorrectly relied upon as the mechanism, but it isn't. The primary relationship for this work is between you and your higher power. Ditto for your partner.

So when things go a little wrong with your partner, you have to look at what the fault was, how it makes you feel and react, and how it affects you both. And then you have to work with your higher power to find a better action for next time. In essence, say you're sorry for something and tell your partner what you believe the better action would be and then do it next time. It's not that easy every time but that must be your goal. And if you have troubling or recurring defects then inventory them properly and take them back to your sponsor. Remember though, a resolution will always come if you work at it.

By the way, sometimes I hear people say that the steps are in a sequence for a reason, and they should only be done in order. I agree with that, for the first couple of years of recovery. But there is also the expression that somebody who is wise "knows something inside-out and back-to-front". I have found that with the steps and other recovery tools such as the serenity prayer, working out for yourself what these things can do when you go through them backwards is very useful. You find additional logic and different ways to use them for even better outcomes. Experience my that's, least at.

Kathryn's and My Joint Step Ten and Our 'Little Spikes'

I now believe that a joint step ten process is critically important for a relationship. Generally, in recovery, when we talk about step ten and 'promptly admitting it', we tend to treat that as something just about ourselves. But in a relationship we are both damaged and flawed and our faults interact – sometimes at considerable depth.

My wife and I have developed ways of doing this that seem to work well for us. But I don't think one particular solution would fit everyone, because the need for it comes from our specific character defects. Here are some of our examples.

Due to some bad experiences in my past, I can sometimes feel threatened when I meet a large group of women. This might be meeting some of my partner's work colleagues (almost all women), or female groups of friends that she has. What happens is this; I believe they are, as a group, judging me – taking the view that I must almost certainly be about to break the love and trust of my partner by cheating, gambling, liking football, drinking, not working, liking rugby or being violent.

Now this is based in some truths all round. Female friends are often left to pick up the pieces after the bad behaviour of a man in a relationship. And at one time, a group of women were left to pick up the pieces from the total mess that I left behind – so I feel shame for that. But also, well into sobriety, with groups of women not in recovery, I feel I've been automatically tarred with the same old brush; just another one of those bad men, even though they don't know me. So I would go quiet and my defences went up. My wife picked up on this a couple of times more recently so we took some action by discussing it at depth, and she could see how not only were my fears groundless but also she saw the incorrect thinking they were based in (the past, sick people, my own active alcoholism back then and so-on). This enabled me to see more of the truth in it and take it to my higher power for a while. Now my fear and incorrect action in a group of women is completely gone - indeed, I could see that my quiet, sometimes prickly demeanour was the real cause of the effect – with normal friendly communication everything is just fine.

My wife has a little defect that comes from her childhood. It's about precious personal possessions that she used to hold onto very dearly when she felt insecure; panicking if she lost something or someone took something away from her. These days, just occasionally, this pops up. The other day she went to set up her laptop in the lounge and the charger wasn't there. We'd had visitors the previous week and I had moved the laptop and charger up to the office, and put the charger safely in a draw with some other cables. Well, she panicked, because in her mind the charger was lost forever and her laptop rendered permanently useless. And this was the second or third time I had seen this, so I gently challenged her to find out what the underlying problem was. Like me with the groups of women, on the surface the behaviour didn't match the situation and there was something from way in the past that, on our own, we couldn't see needed some step ten work.

We've now come to call these things 'spikes'. They're just a little spike left behind from a bigger past hurt or defect. And in a strange way they have turned out to be a blessing because, when we find the courage and grace to talk honestly about them, we both learn something new and important about ourselves. By the way, I have deliberately used these particular examples because they do look a bit nuts in writing. It's all too easy for us to hide these sorts of things because they do seem crazy, but if you have traits like these, you can be sure your parter is going to see them. Analyse them together, even with a bit of humour thrown in, don't bury them because that will lead to misunderstanding and maybe resentment. And you'll feel much more able to step-ten them when they pop back up in the future.

I mentioned one of Kathryn's other spikes in the previous section when I said about Kathryn being late back after a meeting. She used to overly worry that I'd be angry if she was late. Well, that comes from the behaviour of a previous partner, that's left a little spike there.

Step Twelve

Step twelve is your future. Making a constant effort to live in the solution and put other people first is the practical outcome of this step, but the spiritual outcome of step twelve should, I think, lead to one thing – the feeling of joy. It should not feel too hard being this good, it should not be a battle of mistakes and calamity or the feeling of constant fear in the pit of one's stomach. It should be success, with peace, contentment and productivity as major elements of your new life.

But we also talk about the bridge to normal living, so we need to include normal things in our new plans. I know it sounds crazy but sometimes I think people over-indulge in recovery activity. Bill W knew this could happen, which is why he included the concept of normal living. We're not aiming to get to a steady state of good recovery only to live the rest of our lives like we're in a closed religious order. We want to get married, travel and run businesses. But not everyone gets it. Have you ever thought, in AA meetings, how you can clearly see the difference between those who have properly reached step twelve, and those who haven't? What I mean about the difference goes something like this: those who have not reached step twelve include newcomers of course, and those people who are clearly making their way through the steps for the first time. But there are also the serial relapsers, the high-risk two-steppers, those who dwell in their misery, and those who complain constantly about the programme.

Those who have genuinely reached step twelve talk in a different way. They share in meetings to support the theme of the meeting and they do service and sponsor. They have the calmness and humility of having gained genuine wisdom and have some sort of recognisable spiritual awakening in their manner. They also do lots of things outside the fellowship.

And if we look at the people that we know well in recovery, it's usually those who have properly reached step twelve that have successful long-term relationships. Now this is a big thing to think about – what it means is that those who do not have a good spiritual balance are higher-risk relationship material. This is of course why there is that saying not to start a new relationship for the first year of recovery, or that strong warning about thirteen stepping, but those mantras are a rather blunt weapon. Instead why not take people forward into a logical, wisdom-based process to learn about relationships? Now I can hear some people say, it's not the fellowships role to teach about relationships, but in my view that's not the case because relationships are part of 'all our affairs' and present a very high risk to recovery if they go wrong. If you were sponsoring someone and they had major problems at work that was risking their sobriety, you would help them inventory and find ways to change. That surely must be the same for the in-love and sex instincts.

Now let's look at some positive things here too. Obviously I am first suggesting to be cautious – don't forget how risky in-love is, without a good set of tools to balance things out. But equally, if we are more aware of the risks, we can use that knowledge to help find someone more suitable for us. Everyone has flaws and everyone is on their personal journey, and if we want a relationship, we are navigating quite complex terrain. It might be that you meet someone wonderful who is on the early part of their path, and whilst they still have a lot of work to do, maybe together you can be better and stronger. The thing is that neither of you go in blind. Discuss the risks, don't do anything early that is a difficult commitment to get out of. In this case one, or both of you might not have got to step twelve, but ask yourselves honestly, are you working effectively towards it? If so, maybe you can take things forwards slowly.

Chapter Six – Character Defects And The Principles

One of the strange anomalies with the main AA literature is that nowhere does it list the principles that we are supposed to practice. When we get to step twelve, what principles are we referring to? In more recent times, many people have introduced the idea that our individual principles should be the opposites of our own character defects. And this is definitely how I have come to see them – they are the good behaviours that you're trying to achieve in step seven.

Let me explain. Each of us ends up with a list of character defects from our step four inventory, then we work to replace those defects with the opposites in steps six and seven. So if we were dishonest, we try and practice honesty, if we were fearful - courage, arrogance - humility, and so-on. Those things we aim for are our personal principles. The main ones are discussed in every piece of AA literature, and surely they apply to us all, although they are not listed as such. But there will be more specific ones for each of us too. Maybe you're a little agoraphobic, or a bit OCD around the house, or perhaps too easily pick up mini-resentments or overreact with a sharp tongue when criticised. Whatever those things are that you find in yourself, you should end up with a clear idea of what the opposites are for you – your own principles to practice.

In your early days of recovery your principles might be those vitally important concepts of humility and willingness. Or just keeping it in the day, or ninety meetings in ninety days – any form of discipline in your routine at all could be a key principle at the start of recovery. And many of the principles are not specific to any one step, we might first learn about them in a particular step, but we develop them more as we continue forward. They run all the way through the steps, our recovery and into our daily living – and into the core of our relationships.

So our principles start to develop as the opposites of our character defects. And as we go through recovery more of them are revealed to us.

Defects and Principles for Relationships

So as I wrote this book, I developed more and more the idea of what our own character defects are and what our own principles are, for both ourselves as individuals, and for a couple in a relationship. I created large diagrams for this with respect to myself, adding many elements to the overall design. And so the general defects verses principles idea gained clarity. I tried putting them onto something I called a balance diagram with the defects down the left side and the corresponding principles down the right side, with horizontal lines joining each defect to its principle. The idea being that we hopefully are not at the worst end of the scale of our defects, and can never achieve perfection right up at the other end of the scale. We are somewhere along a line between these two ends.

So here is a lists of how I see defects and their principles. The defect is the left hand word, and the counteracting principle is the right hand word. Each description is a combination of how each defect and principle works within us as individuals, and then how it can effect couples in a relationship. And the effects in a relationship can be significantly greater it turns out – again showing how important it is to work this things together, as well as individually.

By the way, this chapter has turned out to be quite 'chunky'. You might find it easier to dip in and out of this listing of defects and principles. Maybe just concentrate on one or two for a while, developing your own take on the issues before coming back for more.

Resentment – Letting Go

Let's first start with resentments. I always think of resentments as the broad process of replaying the tape and not just feeling bitter towards a person. I can get stuck on repeat, watching again some event that I felt was an injustice to my inflated ego. And on repeat, it keeps getting worse and worse, and I think about it more and more, getting more hurt or angry all the time.

The resentment machine prevents proper thinking – it will hijack any useful train of thought, block out your higher power and drain your mental energy. Indeed I have met some folk in the fellowship who literally cannot read a short passage from the big book, or listen to a short share in a meeting without being totally sidetracked halfway through by a major resentment. In this state we cannot learn or do anything useful. So we must stop it. We have to let resentments go and leave them out of reach.

Each resentment has within it someone or something to blame. Maybe that's the key – let go of the blame. That blame is useless, a burden and only damaging to you. Let the blame go like you would let some old clothes go to recycling – you've worn those things until they are threadbare, they look terrible and everyone else can see you should have been rid of them long ago.

If you have learned about the risk of resentments to your sobriety, you should easily see that they present a similar risk to relationships. And not just for those in recovery – I have seen the relationships of supposedly normal people being slowly wrecked by the build-up of resentments. Carrying around a myriad of little resentments reminds me of that funny expression "being nibbled to death by ducks". Little resentments will get you too in the end.

Let's zoom out now and look at the bigger concept of resentment that from it's French origin, means to 're-feel'. All humans get out-of-balance drives from their instincts, particularly the sex and in-love instincts. And these strong drives can get further distorted and amplified in the brain of the alcoholic. The particular issue here I suppose is that we can get carried away or even obsessive about a possible new relationship. Such things can go right or they can go wrong; a perfect romance, a match made in heaven, in each other's pockets, blinded by love, a pest, a hanger-on, a player, easy, a tart, desperate. What these expressions point to is an infatuation or obsession that we don't know what to do with – a form of resentment. Such feelings can often feel great to us, as they're meant to of course – our problem in sobriety is how to keep them in balance and not just keep replaying them. I think the first indication that we might be getting into trouble is to look at how we're thinking about those feelings. For example replaying the last time we saw a person, or imagining what it might be like the next time we meet them, kiss them, maybe even sleep with them. And then we can also look at the effects that might have on us – are we ignoring our friends, being bad at our work, or even reducing our chances of success with our potential new partner by simply not being cool.

So as we wise-up to the broader effects of the replay machine I think we can work out ways to first measure it, then keep it in check. To measure resentment activity I've used a similar approach as I would for the

CHARACTER DEFECTS AND THE PRINCIPLES

basic resentment character defect, except I've broadened it out to capture anything that I spend any significant amount of time thinking about. For example, look at your day and list the five things you've spent the most time thinking about. If those things are relevant and logical then that's okay – a lot of your day spent thinking about receipts and invoices because you need to do your monthly expenses, followed by what you need to pick up from the store on the way home, is fine. But if you've been checking your phone every five minutes to see if someone has replied to a text you sent yesterday, then that probably isn't so good. With relationships, especially when they are only a possibility, it is very easy for us to start over-thinking. But you might say so what? Well the problem is, over-thinking can lead to over-reaction if we're not careful. For example, our emotions might be over-reacting inside, making us feel anxious and stressed, but also we might literally over-react when we are with our potential new partner, perhaps becoming possessive or jealous, even though that might be out of character for us normally.

For me, I can pretty much guarantee that my behaviour will change if I am over-charged with instinct-driven thinking. A couple of times when first courting Kathryn, I mis-read and reacted quite stupidly to a couple of small things that turned out to be absolutely nothing. You know the sort of thing – your anxiety is very high because you want something, and want to impress, but instead you blurt something silly out or don't appear very cool and relaxed. Then I would worry deeply about my silly mistake, thinking more and more about it and how to put it right again. You can soon spiral-in on yourself that way.

And other things can consume our thinking too, such as grief, a sense of futility (ask any AlAnon member about that) or maybe just fantasy about what our lives might be. In any of these cases, we have to push away from them, and work towards the principle of letting them go, or just "letting go". You might perhaps develop your own concept of letting go such as the big red stop sign in front of your face, the serenity prayer, the just for today card or re-reading your inventory. Ultimately you have to use steps six, seven and ten, and get out of self. Do His will not yours, turn to service and help others, and think calmly about the possibility of a wonderful new relationship. In this regard, part of the letting go process is actually patience. If something good is meant to happen (sometimes quickly sometimes slowly), it will.

Deceit – Honesty

We are clearly told at the start of chapter five of the Big Book that a lack of honesty is the biggest block to a successful recovery. Well, if it applies to recovery that directly, how can it be any different for relationships? During our active alcoholism we were never honest about our drinking habits, the money we were wasting, our social disasters, trouble with the law and so-on. That dishonesty was all about enabling our drinking – at any cost. And so much of it was directed at the people close to us – to prevent them stopping us from getting what we wanted. We didn't care about the hurt we caused people, nor any of the consequences for them. To me this is the essence of the cause-and-effect of our dishonesty.

You often hear simple examples in the fellowship about dishonesty, such as when a shopkeeper might give you too much change and you make the good decision to give it back. Yes of course it's good to practice honesty in that way but that scenario doesn't carry any significant impact from the decision either way. Three much more useful examples could be, firstly, the way a child might lie when unexpectedly asked if she took a cookie from the cookie jar, and she answers no, even though she did take one. I think of that as a reactive denial lie. Replace cookies with booze or money for us of course and think how often we would lie reactively when caught. The second scenario is the pre-planned cover-up lie that might be something like pretending not to know why there is no money left in your families' bank account. The third scenario is when you say you're going to do one thing, but intend to do something else instead. This is the pre-planned lie about a future action. This is a very serious defect with a powerful motive behind it that is designed to deceive – hence deceit. For me, I would typically to say to my family that I could not come home tomorrow night because I had a late business meeting, whereas I was actually planning to go to a bar of course.

Deceit is probably the most terrible type of dishonest thinking, and the most damaging for people around us, especially when they are repeatedly on the receiving end of it. And this is why I chose to put deceit as the opposite of honesty – the word points squarely at the problem of deliberately duping other people, organisations (police or courts) and most of all, partners.

Maybe if fear is the corrosive thread of recovery, deceit is the corrosive thread of relationships. Remember, if we are not in a close relationship we can, and often do, afford ourselves some dishonesty and get away with it. I just don't think that's possible in an effective relationship. And that's worth thinking about carefully – are you genuinely prepared to work on a whole new level of honesty for a relationship?

When we look at the dictionary definitions of deceit we will see how the word means concealing or distorting the truth for the purpose of misleading, cheating or fraud, or making someone believe something that is not true. And that starts to reveal another problem. In addition to the deceit we plan to do, there is also deceit that is invisible to us – the deceit we unknowingly conceal from ourselves. Step five of the Twelve and Twelve talks about all the ways we can be self deceiving in our inventory work, and this is why it's so important to work closely with a sponsor – we just can't see some of our deepest dishonesty without help.

So when it comes to deceit, maybe it's worth each of us actually just inventorying that, right through all our actions and thinking. And we replace it with honesty, the sort of honesty that comes from the will of our higher power – genuine, strong, with courage but also with love and kindness.

Denial – Acceptance

Acceptance is another one of those fundamental threads that runs right through recovery. We soon learn the importance of accepting our alcoholism. And we hear many discussions about acceptance, tolerance and not judging, and it all makes sense for a while, until you start to wonder why people seem to have to work so hard at it. What's slightly strange is that people use tolerance as a mechanism for acceptance and look at the problem from the angle of tolerating things, usually other people. The issue with this is when you tolerate something, you still feel negatively about it, you're just overriding that negativity with an action or attitude that isn't really genuine.

Then when it comes to the basics of denial, a good place to start is how we accept or deny things that are said about us. The most useful dictionary definition to consider here is 'denial is the refusal to admit the truth or reality of something'. And in this context it means not being able to accept something negative about ourselves. This is the damage that a big ego or too much fear inflicts upon us and it comes to the fore when someone else points out our defects.

The way out of it of course is to start practising acceptance. But be careful, we can kid ourselves into thinking we have good acceptance when we help an abusive newcomer, but how well do we do when our partner points out our deepest shortcomings? We start by learning to become teachable from the people in our meetings, from AA literature and our sponsor. We know we have to do most of the things they suggest, or else we are lost. Then, later, we work up to the position where we can accept the uniquely personal input from a partner. For example, can we take criticism with good grace or do we stand our ground in stubbornness and retaliate with aggression? We shouldn't have blind acceptance of unjustified criticism of course, but your bathroom habits or dislike of shopping is something your fellow AAs don't usually experience – but a partner will. So criticism comes from a broader base in a personal relationship – so we need to be prepared with better acceptance skills.

I think in any good relationship you have to establish what works for you in this regard. We talk about a relationship requiring trust and it's here that the trust has to be very high. Trust to include what you think of each other's behaviour into the broader pool of advice, guidance and teaching that we allow into our lives. For me I have found that I have to do it that way – I can't separate what Kathryn suggests I look at from what maybe my sponsor would say, by having any difference in my attitude towards it. If I have any difference in my attitude, that will develop into a filter, driven by denial.

And that interface has to be two way, kind, and loving. We sometimes talk of joy, but perhaps don't often experience it. Well I can give you a great example of joy. In a relationship, we can replace the feelings of friction, worry or lack of honesty about discussing each others defects with one of openness, safety and change together – this is a joyous thing. It takes effort, you have to work at it, it might draw many tears but as you practice, those tears will change to laughter, comfort and here's the biggest one – deep emotional security. And for me, not only is this the core of my marriage, but a huge part of my own spiritual awakening.

So what about the left and right hand ends of this denial/ acceptance line? In a relationship, either one or both people operating at the left hand end is going to be very difficult. We can never have honesty and comfort there. And look at joint humility at this point too – do you collectively have enough humility to admit and change everything? In a way, the right hand end is where you aim for God's perfect acceptance of everyone and everything. And we try to bring that level of humility to our self-acceptance too. Remember how the just for today card points at never criticising others, only trying to change or regulate ourself? But as in a good team, or in a good relationship, you're walking down that street together, each one trying to keep his or her own side of it clean, but also helping with the other side too.

Arrogance and Pride – Humility

Pride is a difficult thing to understand. In British English we tend to only mention pride for the feeling we get when either we or those around us have a simple success. "I'm proud of my son for winning the race", or "I'm proud of myself for a good job in the garden." At this level it's pretty harmless. But what about the pride that's listed as a deadly sin, or the pride that supposedly comes before a fall? And what about arrogance? The dictionary says arrogance is an exaggerated opinion of oneself as expressed to others. And then, how is humility the antidote to pride and arrogance?

My own thoughts go like this. We first learn that humility is about deflating our ego and getting right sized – something in my early years I never really understood. But there's a good description of Bill W's that I like, in which he is on a grassy path with the bog of fear, guilt and remorse on one side, and the "gold coins" of pride and arrogance on the other. And humility in this analogy is staying on that good path and not deviating either left or right. Ah, I can start to get it now – the bad things like guilt and fear I can see easily, and I must keep away from them. I must leave them over there, way out to the left of my path. But arrogance and pride are now clear entities too. The tricky thing is they don't at first look so bad. But they're there, out to the right of my path and I learn I must keep away from them. Bill lists prideful things (his gold coins) such as greed, power or status, that can lead us back into danger as easily as fear or guilt.

In my early sobriety I got the general point of the story but never felt I suffered much from pride. But later I began to see hints of it in me, and some of the people around me. What we seem to do is form a distorted attitude to a piece of knowledge or an opinion that we hold. The incorrect idea is usually about ourselves in some way, and the attitude that goes with it is one of either exaggeration or denial. Then an inflated ego kicks in, one that believes our distorted opinion is correct and that we should take some important action because of it – telling ourselves, or other people, to believe in or do something based on our erroneous idea. And if we don't have enough honesty, are not cured of self deception, we will become defensive if we are challenged on our view, genuinely not accepting a more sensible counter-argument when we hear it.

In recovery, this is the form of pride that stops us taking important advice from our sponsor, or creates a belief that we can't relate to other members of the fellowship because they just don't see it our way. And we all know people in recovery who have that one really dangerous piece of pride, where they believe they surely must have the power to beat the drinking game by themselves.

One night in a meeting, the topic of arrogance, pride and humility was on the table, and as we went through the meeting we collectively came up with some very interesting descriptions using the idea of opposites. One person shared that the opposite of humility was arrogance, and described how we could unjustly criticise another with hurtful comments, such as stating the other person's status or opinion was inferior to our own, and then go on to tell the other person exactly how our way would be an improvement they ought to follow. We are arrogant toward that other person and it's an outward process. Then someone else described how they puffed up their chest with pride after reaching three months sobriety, then nearly ended up in a bar to celebrate the success. They had a falsely positive opinion of their own ability and this is an inward process.

So in a way pride and arrogance are a form of fantasy, in that they are based in a lack of reality. And where pride is a lack of reality about ones own importance and abilities in a largely passive 'inward-looking' way, arrogance takes that same sense of over importance (fantasy), but aims it squarely at other people. Arrogance is usually combined with unjust criticism and lack of acceptance of other people.

Coming back to humility, in the case of recognising and stopping injustice and falsehood in ourselves, we should take humility on board as quite a specific good principle to practice. We see the stupidity and unkindness of pride and arrogance and we make a decision to stop it. But humility also brings in the concept of being on the right path, and staying on that path in order to avoid all the hazards we can so easily fall into.

These things must become central to building a good relationship of course. Like so many other defects, we're more closely exposed to the problems of pride and arrogance when we're in a relationship. The journey to good humility, seen as a path, is no different from the journey to building a good relationship. Indeed, in a relationship, life gets more complex, more emotional and more risky in some ways so we need to double-down on the effort to avoid the hazards either side of our path – handy then that in a relationship there are two of you to share the work.

Fraudulent Behaviour – Esteemable Behaviour

When I first started writing about this principle I called it Fraud versus Esteem. But that did not put the correct behavioural focus on it. Fraud is often associated with criminal financial activity, but that idea is misleading in this context. The area I'm thinking of is in the way we might call a person a fraud, because they are not what they seem.

Fraudulent behaviour links closely to deceit I think, but it probably broadens out to cover more things. In essence it is a character defect that stops us revealing who we really are. It's very dangerous if we don't look at this in our recoveries because it prevents us being honest enough in our own step work and also poses a great risk to relationships. Pretending to be something we're not, in a relationship, is deceitful of course. But here's the thing, because of the power of our instincts it's sometimes very difficult for us not to behave like this – we show off, big ourselves up when we're dating, not a major problem if you just come across as a plonker, but what if we mask a poor financial situation, our marital status, a criminal record or something else serious? Well the simple answer is we don't have the right to be that irresponsible towards another human being, particularly if we are expecting to create a serious relationship with someone. We must be transparent to the reality of our situation.

Fraudulent behaviour could be people pleasing or being boastful about our achievements. Or more seriously, actively trying to feed our own egos by putting other people down. Some folks would call that scoring points and it's very selfish and hurtful. Sometimes you might see this in the fellowship itself, where people become competitive or evangelical about their recovery knowledge and ideas.

Then there's esteem. You often hear "if you want esteem, do estimable things". If you have esteem from others, in essence people respect and value you, and from that it would follow that you then get self-esteem. It's a funny thing though, to do things to get esteem sounds like that process, in itself, would therefore lack humility. But if you always try to do the right thing and put other's first for genuine reasons, work hard and so-on, people will be appreciative of it. So a good way of looking at esteem is other people having genuine gratitude for the selfless and constructive actions you carry out, and that you really are what you say you are.

And it really has to be genuine. I heard a great share once from someone who described the idea of bad motives sitting beneath good ones. This in essence is appearing to do good things to gain esteem but in a selfish way – there is a second motive underneath that is actually using the good things to deflect from bad things in other areas, or perhaps, to subtly fuel an ego, or to convince someone to go out with you.

Doubt – Faith

In our society, faith is normally taken to mean religious faith. But as soon as you put it opposite doubt, it takes on additional meaning.

We talk in recovery about being paralysed with fear, guilt and remorse, or lashing out with rebellion and anger. As part of the antidote we are encouraged to have faith. But the big question is faith in what, or whom, and what does it mean when we do have faith? So, I think we don't develop the concept of faith very well, and I often see it tripping people up in their recovery, usually with a reaction like "oh no, you're saying I have to believe in God!"

In our drinking days we are totally dishonest and we don't rely on anything – the only certainty we have is that if we drink we get drunk. We don't take any advice from friends, doctors and counsellors. We won't believe that what they say would be better for us and react in a rebellious or defiant way usually. Then we reach our rock bottom and become broken and desperate for a way out. On the day we walk into our first meeting, all we usually have is an uneasy sense that we're in some form of imminent danger.

As soon as we start to hear all that recovery speak, it sounds like gibberish, the process seems impossible in our minds at that time. So we form an almost zero belief that it can work – we doubt it hugely. Belief is the same as faith to me, and with recovery, it's primarily finding belief that there will be a positive result even though we have not experienced it yet. In our AA literature we read "came to believe", and that implies a timescale. We talk about handing our will and our life over to the care of a higher power so that something can happen – later. In meetings and with our sponsors we talk about doing inventories and changing character defects, and about having faith that we can change all these things, and have a good and worthwhile life developing, over time.

Well, if we don't believe any of that will work for us then we lack faith. That lack of faith is a character defect in its own right – or really, excessive doubt is the character defect.

So when you consider how doubt functions within you, in your mind, try and analyse the thinking at depth. Maybe you tend to disregard things out of hand because it suits an agenda. Saying to yourself that you doubt something is an easy way to avoid effort to take action – a habit quite a lot of people have about all sorts of aspects in life. Even the silly expression "if it sounds too good to be true, it probably is" gets used as a sarcastic way of avoiding whole hearted buy-in. Instead, remember that "it works *if* you work it" – is really saying it will work if you have faith that it will work. Don't give your brain an exit-route of doubt because it will take that way out every time.

And then when it comes to relationships, you hear people bark at each other "you should have more faith in me!" But again that comment is usually not based on any understanding of faith, or discussion and agreement between two people on how much they intend to rely on each other in an honest and consistent way. If we did put in place good processes that lead to faith in each other, we would remove any significant doubt that the other person might not do the right thing. And then we make more effort, and the relationship gets better. It's exactly the same mechanism as recovery.

Anger – Grace

God's grace, to me, means infinite tolerance and understanding, with total acceptance. And absolutely no adverse reaction to anything. Anger to me feels like an uncontrolled reaction, an elevation of negative emotions because I don't like the way something is. Those emotions are usually outward reactions that mean I might become abusive or argumentative. I might fume inside, burn-up then let it all out in a flurry of bad temper. Or maybe I will sulk and brood over it, take it out on other's in a negative or passive-aggressive way.

The Big Book describes how anger is the dubious luxury of normal folk, but something us alcoholics cannot indulge in. Perhaps, second to picking up a drink, a big outburst of anger points at a poor spiritual condition. An angry outburst will make others reel away from us, retaliate in kind, or even plan a counter-attack. And in a relationship it's this counter-attack response that's the worst outcome. A battle within a relationship, fuelled by anger is a terrible thing. I think that any relationship which has angry rows is a long way from the level of mutual grace that's required for success.

So, for recovering alcoholics who want a relationship, the work on reducing anger and replacing it with grace is a major task. I started with a few obvious techniques to help me with this process, such as taking a deep breath or making a cup of tea whilst I forced myself inside to not release the feeling of anger. Then as I built up better conscious contact with my higher power, I pictured him standing by my side, his loving but strong eye-contact with me clearly saying that his grace was the antidote to my anger. And I look back at him and perhaps think of how Jesus behaved so forgivingly towards the Romans at the end of his life – without anger. That example always quickly brings me back in the direction of grace.

I think every couple should work on anger together. Maybe make it as equally off-limits as drinking or cheating – I think for relationships, anger really is that dangerous.

Guilt – Forgiveness

I think we all know what our type of guilt is. That flashback to the past and the stomach-churning feeling that goes with it as we re-live the foolish things we did. Or, when people remind us of the damage we caused them and how it sickens us to see that things can never be the same again. It's a harsh one this, it can really hurt. We always have to dig deep to counteract it. In the area of relationships, the past-damage-score and guilt that goes with it is likely to be high.

Then in recovery we learn about acceptance. We have to accept the wreckage of our past and must not be crippled by it now. As we grow, we see that we can in a way, change the effect of the past – how we see it and feel it. When we look back at something now, we have confidence we wouldn't do anything like that again. We hear many old-timers say "we know something now we didn't know before." In essence, we know how our rampaging character made us behave before, but we don't have to do that now.

But where does forgiveness come in? Firstly, when we look back we can see that we didn't know how to behave any better. I look back at myself and see a different person. I was sick then, I was the raging alcoholic, the troublemaker, the destroyer of things. Just as when a newcomer comes into the rooms, we should not hold ourselves in contempt for the way we behaved when drinking. We care for newcomers, and ourselves – we gain a deeper understanding of things because not only have we been there, but because we've been through the process that brings results. We understand it, and we hold no blame against others, or ourselves for what happened – we forgive.

But forgiveness is a principle that requires further development in the area of relationships. The requirement for forgiveness can be on a different scale. When two people become close, a lot of smaller low-level differences are going to be revealed. Note I say differences rather than defects here – an important differentiation to avoid trying to inventory every little domestic issue. With these sorts of things you can work out a process of responsibility, (own the issue), acceptance and forgiveness. Talk about your differences in a lighthearted way to see what you can change. With things that perhaps you can't change easily – do little work-arounds. This all has to be done in a loving way with gentle compromises and lots of acceptance. Change things in yourself that suit the other person better. Be giving and gentle and be mindful that if this is done well it can be a gateway into a new sort of relationship – one where each day is not a journey through grumpy comments, subtle disapproval and a lack of acceptance when something small goes wrong. In essence, we must not have a constant background mood which lacks forgiveness.

At the other end of the scale, sometimes a partner may do things that harm us greatly. Infidelity and violence are two that spring to mind.

These harms originate in serious character defects that if left unchecked will keep creating more harms. In such situations the guilty partner may seek our forgiveness, perhaps repeatedly or even quite forcibly – turning it around that you are at fault because you cannot forgive. This is just one example, but it highlights that mistakes require responsibility and proper solutions, so that the need for the initial forgiveness gets replaced by gratitude for us having made things genuinely better. A cycle of serious harm and forgiveness-seeking is not sustainable in any healthy relationship and must be seen as crossing a line of acceptability for your own happiness and wellbeing. If this is so, hit the serenity prayer hard and make new plans accordingly.

Fear – Courage

All the way through the steps we are taught about fear and how it affects us. Most of us are incredibly fearful when we first try to admit we are alcoholic – that bereft sort of fear that's driven by the total lack of hope and deep shame about our situation. Finding out that we are not the only one suffering from this illness starts to help and once we commence sorting out our basic affairs, the fears caused by unmanageability begin to reduce too.

But as we progress into recovery we find that we're constantly hit by fear, and what's so troubling is we can see how drink used to be our antidote. So now we're not drinking, we're totally exposed. And this is where we need to find that first piece of true courage – courage to change the things we can always means, at first, not to be so frightened. How? Unfortunately, just holding on tight and going with it is our only option at the start. You've got to find courage to get into that roller-coaster carriage. I remember listening to people in my early meetings and thinking the only choice I seem to have is to hope that they're telling the truth, or go back to drinking.

Once we get into the steps proper, we start taking inventories. Usually we inventory resentments, fears, harms and sex conduct. And we learn a simple definition of fear in general, that we fear losing something we have, or fear not getting something we want. So the emotion comes from either loss, or not having, and it's important to understand that we get such a heightened sense of these two things from our basic alcoholism – if someone took our drink away or we couldn't get the drink we want. That specific fear became our one and only emotional experience.

Another basic thing that creates fear, that is not identified so clearly I think, is making effort. If we're honest about ourselves we will see countless examples where we're fearful of making genuine effort to do the right thing. We might see what's required, but do we do it? We know it's a programme of action but if we examine what happens when we try to take action, try to find the energy and motivation to do it, we often feel fear. We might also feel insecure or under-confident about doing things, or even, quite simply, be lazy. Sloth is a deadly sin. We are fearful of action for many reasons.

This is where we need to start working on courage. If we want to find courage to do things, we need to try our best to throw off the fear of action. There is still the odd time when I have to try and deny myself any significant feelings about a difficult task or action, or else those emotions might stop me. The fear might be based around doubt in my ability or what other people think. If those thoughts do creep in, I put up my big red stop sign and decide that if the basic value of the action is good, then I must just go for it. But that's not always easy when it's a big action; sometimes I fail in the process. So this is where a meeting, a sponsor, a higher power or a great partner comes in – an external input that restores your confidence and gives you courage again.

CHARACTER DEFECTS AND THE PRINCIPLES

The idea that courage comes from both inside and out is important I think. This is well known in the military where soldiers are trained hard, pushed to their limit so they experience and get used to their own fear, and then go on to defeat those fears with high levels of courage. When each person's individual courage gets to its limits, then it becomes the collective courage of the squad or platoon, the guidance under fire from the experienced sergeant say, who perhaps with one or two simple words, calms them all. The chain of command, the teamwork and knowing that your pal is covering your back take away fear. Reliance on each other, trust in each others' abilities, good judgement and even love is the essence of it all. And love? Yes, the bond of love in a close-nit military unit is high and it's there for one purpose – to find the courage to take action.

When it comes to relationships there are a lot of instinct driven fears to consider. Our instincts can produce fear in us or fear in others. Perhaps the best example is, again, jealousy. There is a big difference between the fear of losing a job and the fear of losing your partner to a younger, much more handsome man who has a better car and job than you, and whom everyone thinks is cool, and who just keeps hanging around your partner making her laugh and smile... Feels different huh?

Yes, you might feel jealous, but are you reading the situation right? Jealousy is designed for reproductive competition, it wants me and smarty-pants over there to fight for my gal. It want's me to feel bad, to feel affronted, challenged, belittled. It wants me to feel fear, then rage, and go over there and sort him out. Gladly. Allow this sort of behaviour though, and you're likely to not get the results your fear driven reaction is designed for. First, this fear based reaction (some would call it an irrational fear) is often wrong in its perception of the situation. We very quickly jump to the wrong conclusion. And second, if we start over-reacting to things like this around a good partner, we will almost certainly start generating fear in that person about our behaviour.

In a relationship, fear at the personal level generally seems to grow from a lack of trust. We have to be very clear that we need to build trust between each other as clearly as any other fundamentals we have to live by. But of course we are often so damaged from a shaky past that for some of us it can be hard to trust. That is where the courage comes in – courage to trust the person we love.

Of course I'm only scratching the surface here. Our deep understanding about fear and courage has to come from the core of our recovery work. But I have found from my own experience that a good relationship should be part of that work. Like all the other principles, you can look at fear and courage on its left hand/right hand scale. And then we can work to move right on that line. Remember that one of the greatest gifts you can give a partner, just like the soldiers under fire, is the type of love that leads to courage. Then they can defeat their greatest fears.

Threat – Surrender

Threat, or more specifically when and how we feel threatened, goes back to our very basic instincts.

Let me give you a strange example. In the audio industry (something I know a little about) some serious enthusiasts have specially-built listening rooms with all sorts of fancy acoustic absorbers on the walls. When listening in one of these rooms, a friend explained a very interesting aspect about the rear wall. It had been designed to stop sound waves reflecting back at you from behind. Why? Well, reflections can pollute the sound of course, but he went on to say that if we hear little sounds coming from behind us, it triggers our natural threat defences. Sub-consciously we think a tiger or something is sneaking around behind us, so we're at a heightened threat state that is much less relaxing, even disconcerting. But take away the rear reflections and you really do feel much more peaceful as you sit there listening to the music.

Have you noticed that with some of our own character defects, particularly those that might make us feel self-conscious, or inferior, or less intelligent than others, you get a strange uneasy feeling, or perhaps you feel offended and the hairs on the back of your neck stand up? I think that reaction is a threat response. It might be that you are being put-down by someone who isn't very nice, or you are being threatened by a difficult situation. But as your recovery develops and you sweep away the real threats, we can still be left with a lot of imaginary ones. People might say we're doing well, or we're great, or that they love us but we might not believe them. We might feel threatened because in the past people might have said those things but not meant them. We're over-sensitive of course.

A relationship can be a minefield of perceived threats. When a partner criticises us even mildly, we can get that threatened feeling strongly, which makes us quick to defend ourselves, or even retaliate. A partner might then say that awful phrase "you're being defensive" – and off it goes. We hate that phrase being directed at us but then, how many times have we used it on others? So it's worth taking a good look at the threat and defence processes in our relationships.

Then we can employ the principle of surrender, as long as it doesn't put us at risk. When a situation arrises that appears to be a threat, makes us feel defensive, we want to be able to see how our reaction in those situations is undesirable – we want to replace that undesirable reaction with surrender.

Maybe it's like when soldiers surrender when they know they are losing a battle and there's no way out. They are told by their officers to stop fighting the enemy and they relinquish command of their troops to the enemy. This is an admission of complete defeat, that your side has no way of winning, perhaps no way of even feeding its soldiers any more. The only option is to ask the other side to take over the responsibility for the needs of your people and hope that they will feed and shelter them.

So fighting a threat, or surrendering to it, is a decision. Unfortunately most of us are programmed through our alcoholism to usually make the wrong decision here. If we're honest we can see so many times where we fought the perceived threat, stood our ground, didn't give in, argued the toss, or as the Americans say, we had a fight. We all know that feeling, when we feel we can't give-in because it seems like a humiliation. But if you're in a good relationship with a good person, just surrender instead, and see what happens. Don't do it for sympathy or drama, do it gently and constructively. Talk about how your reaction is usually to defend rather than surrender and that you want to change that. Make it safe to surrender for both of you of course, admit your faults together and love each other as you practice this principle.

Selfishness – Service

I often think of the St Francis prayer when I think of service. I like the way it lists things to 'sow', with a sense of location – where there is hatred, sow love, where there is despair sow hope etc. Then the second part of the prayer lists things that we should not seek for ourselves but should give to others – its better to love than be loved, or its better to... And at the end it says, in essence, it's through giving that we receive Gods love. To me it's that feeling when you know you've done the right thing.

It's a hard thing to hold onto though, that feeling of receiving love through doing the right thing. Our own selfish defects so swiftly sweep the feeling aside. But here's a little trick I sometimes say to sponsees when they're in a situation and are finding it hard to stop reacting selfishly to something – I ask them what would Jesus do? I tell them to think back to when they were in school, maybe about eight or nine years old, and are being taught one of the parables about Jesus. Perhaps Jesus is helping those with illness, or those living in poverty, and he's doing so without any judgement or limit to his effort. Strangely, when we think of this, we can imagine that purity of heart, and that Jesus is doing Gods will with absolute grace and love. When I then say, "so what would Jesus do if he was in your situation right now", the sponsee nods with a knowing smile that Jesus certainly wouldn't react with the resentment or anger that they are feeling, that Jesus would bring peace and harmony to the situation as best he could, with only thoughts of the wellbeing of others. You can do this with any situation, and somehow it helps to think back to those stories about Jesus. Try asking yourself the same question when you are confronting something tricky – it's quite hard not to get the right answer – to see the selfless action that is required.

So then selfishness, I guess, is doing anything that does not follow this idea. Whether you believe in God, Jesus, or any higher power, you could also think of your sponsor, that teacher you liked back at school – or even a character in a movie. Yes, think how we like the good-guy in a movie – we watch the good and bad guys play out the story and it's so easy to see the selfless actions of the good characters and we love them for it. If you can start to see into your own defects in the same way, identify without self-deception where you are putting yourself unnecessarily first, then you are on the path to becoming the hero/heroine (and the one that gets the girl or boy in the end).

In a relationship, two people being appropriately unselfish is, strangely, quite a hard balance to find. But I think it gets considerably easier if you use the concept of service as the opposite to selfishness. All those things you need to do in a relationship can start to fall under the banner of service. Running the house, raising the kids, having lovely days out (sober), a good sex life.

Do you notice how, when we get married we all make wedding vows? We solemnly say those vows that in a way are the same as many of the principles we are talking about here, yet how many of us so quickly forget them? We know now, that to maintain any principles we have to practice them every day, whether they're based in the twelve steps or wedding vows – apply them and you're going to be much happier, that's for sure.

Thinking about those vows, or all the selfless things Jesus did, it's all about serving others – doing service. Funny how we call worship at church a service, or even how we might say we had good service from a certain shop assistant in a store. Oh, one little thing about our St Francis prayer. Turns out the prayer didn't come from St Francis at all. It was written much later (1900's), by Franciscan nuns in Paris.

Chaos – Peace

The dictionary describes chaos as utter confusion or disorder. And chaos theory in science is the study of chaotic systems, or how the universe might be sensitive to the way it was when it started… or something like that, who knows.

But chaos for active alcoholics is the way we create 'our tornado'. Breaking friendships, losing all our money, ending up in jail or hospital. Wrecked relationships and poor job prospects, nowhere to live and no friends. This might be where we've ended up when we hit our rock bottom. Hopefully that all starts to turn around when we find recovery, but our natural state is to create chaos. So we have to work to balance it out.

Chaos in a relationship means big trouble. If we are chaotic we sap energy from the relationship – goodwill and affection are drained. We won't be reliable or make good plans. We may seem almost deliberately destructive at times. Even if we say we are in good recovery, others around us begin to doubt it.

I suppose on a grand scale, peace is the opposite to war, (maybe when drinking we resembled a war-zone). But, I think the sort of peace we are after is a state of calmness, thoughtfulness and consideration. You sometimes hear people use the expression "keeping the peace", and they mean in a family or relationship situation – it's when someone is making a deliberate effort to stop other people behaving badly.

So peace as a principle is a very good one to work towards. Discuss it with your sponsor first perhaps, and do a mini-inventory on your thinking and actions and look for any chaotic behaviour. Look for practical actions that need doing that you keep putting off – household jobs not finished for example can feel hugely frustrating to those around you. Work on it with your partner and honestly assess together how your relationship could have more peace. In a way you can link it to other principles like acceptance or grace, whatever works best for you to avoid the risk of chaos in your relationship.

But what if it's your partner that creates all the chaos? Maybe that will be one of the factors when considering if the relationship should continue or not. We sometimes hear old-timer's say "avoid vexatious people" and "don't let some people (who brings chaos) cross the threshold of your door." It can be a harsh one this, to make a decision about, but we're after lots of peace here – that isn't going to happen unless both of you in a relationship live your lives peacefully.

And watch out that you don't become a perpetual peacemaker. There can be times in our recovery, when we have big family issues, feelings of huge guilt or trying to make big amends, that we want to fix everything including the relationships between other people. Or we might be trying to support other people emotionally or maybe financially, who should really be left to stand on their own feet. Those people need to become peaceful themselves, you will never bring that about by your actions alone.

Depression – Wellbeing

One of the big things we aim for in recovery is serenity. We talk about it an awful lot in meetings. It's a beautiful, if sometimes rather fleeting feeling of no cares and no worries – peace of mind. By removing a lot of unmanageability, and character defects, we can start to gain some serenity. But sometimes serenity seems rather spiritual in its concept; what about how we're doing in a more general way? When I talked earlier about the established recovery cycle, I said that at the left hand end lies depression. The line goes, in essence, from depression at the left, towards wellbeing at the right. And by the way, I'm taking wellbeing as literally meaning 'being well', as in not sick - in any department of our lives, and depression means depressed as in 'below a normal level'. We say things like "the economy is depressed" or, "the country is in a depression" which means the economy is in a dramatic downturn with a sharp fall in growth, employment and productivity. Sound familiar? That's very similar to when we inventory ourselves as a going-concern, or a store, with bad stock in trade that we have to replace with good. When we look at depression like this it takes the business analogy, the business of living, a lot further.

Wellbeing needs a lot more planning and structure than simple serenity can provide. An example I often see is when folk go to an AA convention, (a weekend affair say). They settle into it, get a real spiritual blast and say they are finding a lot of serenity – that vanishes within about 24 hours of getting home again. When you examine more deeply how the convention affected them, it often comes from the shares from those people who have made great changes in the structure of their lives. The 'winners' who get asked to share at conventions have a lot of wellbeing that underpins their serenity. We can feel it. But then most of us go home and fail to make the drastic changes that those people shared about.

Perhaps at this point I should explain why I have not gone into any debate about clinical depression. I'm sure there's some truth in the medical view that brain chemical imbalances can result in significant problems. I'm not qualified, but also I'm not convinced. I'm afraid what I discover with most people I meet is that their 'depression' is of the spiritual and life-structure kind. Fortunately, more recently, there have been great developments in understanding with new papers being published and discussed in psychology journals. In essence these papers, put forward by anthropologists (those who study human societies and cultures), propose a total rethink, suggesting that depression and many other conditions are responses to adversity and not chemical imbalances at all. That to me sounds much more like the 'reaction to adversity' type of depression suffered by alcoholics.

Turning more broadly to my concept of wellbeing, it's a mistake to think of the recovery cycle lines (Chapter 5) only in terms of removing defects, spiritual progress and so-on. We should do other things too, to get ourselves up the line. One great place to start is in the physical domain. In early recovery we are often a mess physically – both in our physical environment and our bodies. Take a look at all the things you could improve there, your house, your clothes, your hair, your fitness. And also, the physical element means all the people we interact with – so call up an old friend and improve your relationship with them.

I personally put quite a lot of importance on physical fitness and the way I dress. With greater fitness I feel well and strong, I get less fatigue and feel more motivated. I feel more attractive too. I often talk to people about fitness, saying that it absolutely improves your recovery, and relationship prospects too. If you want to feel some wellbeing, wait until someone comments on you looking better, happier and more content – or perhaps even flashes you one of those lovely smiles that suggest they just might find you attractive. Don't get this wrong though, I don't mean we're going to turn into supermodels, but someone who is looking after themselves is attractive to someone else out there. Be confident but cool about it - attraction rather than promotion has a very direct meaning here.

There are many more areas that can be worked on in the same way. I'm sure you can easily identify them. Be productive, and when it comes to wellbeing in a relationship you can work on those things that improve the other persons wellbeing. It's honestly not rocket science but its surprising how many couples never discover that one of the keys to a good relationship is action to improve the other person's wellbeing.

Worry – Contentment

I think there are two main types of worry. There's the worry about something that might or might not happen in the future, and there's the worry that we're not good enough.

Worry is a sort of resentment. It's a re-thinking process – there's something there, in our mind, that we keep going over and over. But it's a little different to other types of over-thinking. Something that we worry about is usually beyond our control, doesn't require any direct action at all or hasn't even happened yet. We can get in a total spin, worrying about everything. We compare ourselves to others and judge ourselves badly in the process, or we project and catastrophise about some future possible event. This sort of thinking often needs deep inventory work and well-structured change, and I think it helps to look at the two types of worry separately.

CHARACTER DEFECTS AND THE PRINCIPLES

We all have not-good-enough worry when we first go to meetings. It's inside us – and through the fog of fear and pain, we worry if we can ever become like the other recovering fellows in the rooms. We have, through our drinking days, always been judged, mostly badly and for good reason, but also judged unfairly many times too. We also at this point really don't know ourselves at all – not what God has intended for us at least. We struggle to learn the steps. We try to comprehend serenity and spiritual living and it's all very hard. Then some of our fears turn to the process of comparison. We compare what we think we are like, to others in recovery. What our lives are like for real and what we think our lives should be. So our friends and sponsor teach us to be right sized, to have humility and to understand what we are. But our minds will make comparisons – we will judge ourselves – all the time. And we will make our shortcomings huge in our minds, and don't see our achievements. We keep on thinking about these things. We worry about them.

This part of the recovery process, the right sized thinking, starts to point us to the principle we should use to combat worry. The principle is contentment, but let's develop that more as we go on.

To deal with future-worry we could say, "those things in the future that could hurt me, but may or may not happen, well, I just won't think about them". But this is not replacing the problem, it's only trying to stop it, (and as we know, that doesn't work very well over time). So let's turn to our higher power. The core spiritual tool of faith is the primary thing for us to use, if and when our worst future-worries come true. The faith is, if something goes wrong, God will help us through it. We worry about our health, our family, our job and our recovery. But what we need to practice is that those worries are a waste of time because God will protect us if the worst should happen.

Here's another thing. We usually have, in the moment, just for today, right here and now, good things all around us. So we can use all those things to replace worry. We should become content with the things we have today and learn to focus on them, rather than on our worries (mindfulness anyone?). Keep reminding yourself, again and again, that worry is just projecting about things that really, most likely, are not going to happen. It starts to look daft when we go at it like this.

So, if contentment is the principle to beat worry, work on contentment. Start doing more things in the day that are good. Service, work, meeting friends or a good afternoon of fun in the bedroom. As you have more of these things in the day, it will start to push out worry. And if a worry does suddenly spring to mind, step ten it then and there, do something to replace it. Friends say things like "let's go shopping, that'll take your mind off it". Parters might say "darling, everything is going to be alright, we'll manage absolutely fine no matter what happens, now let's go for a romantic walk".

In relationships of course, managing worry is part of the teamwork of building wellbeing. If a parter has worries, take action yourself to remove them or minimise the possible impact. Make good decisions and keep being constructive and you can slowly knock each worry off the list, and build your contentment together.

Pain – Joy

I have a long scar on my left shin from a drunken attempt to jump across a storm ditch, onto an open-step steel fire escape, in the dark, with dew on the step. On contact with the step my shoe gave no grip on the wet metal, and my shin went straight into the front of the step above. I then slowly staggered up to bed where I crashed-out without any real awareness of the state I was in. I awoke in the morning to find the sheet stuck to my leg by a large amount of solidified blood. And it hurt like hell. Pain – self inflicted by a bad action.

When I wrote that business case for the church in Wales, it was a lot of work. But I must have done it well enough because the church got the mortgage and soon after, moved into the new building. When my wife and I visited more recently, we were treated like royalty, shown all the new facilities, clubs and a fantastic new control desk for the sound and lighting. Everyone was grinning at us, and my wife didn't quite know what to make of it. "All this (their arms aloft) is because of Steve's amazing business case" they said. I choked-up with joy, having to work hard to hold back the tears in the face of the direct outpouring of gratitude towards me. And it lifted me to the heavens. Joy – self inflicted by a good action.

So it seems to me that one of the main arbiters of pain or joy is a matter of choice. If you chose to do bad things, then a lot of them will result in pain. Pain for you and pain for other people. Do good things and one of the outcomes will be more joy. Seems obvious, yes? But many people don't make decisions that will lessen pain and increase joy.

Perhaps it's worth thinking about the difference between wellbeing and joy here. Wellbeing is supported by a sense of safety and stability, it's a steady constant of contentment, not something that's going to blow your socks off. Perhaps joy is shorter and sharper – like a physical pain that jolts you, joy is a blast. Or maybe a reward? On a recent Caldey Island retreat one of the monks talked at length about the joy of creation and how the nature on the island would fill him with joy as the sun went down on a lovely summer's evening. He didn't feel that feeling strongly all the time – just every now and then, in the moment.

When you connect with something that's really good, that's when you feel it. I think it has to be something really noble and worthwhile. Funny though, how we think of getting involved with something good and worthwhile like a great charity or support group, yet we might not be so selective when choosing a potential partner. So ask yourself the tough questions here, is the partner in your life noble and worthwhile enough to bring you joy? If not, are you going to change that? And also, are you noble and worthy enough in return? By the way, I'm using noble here as defined in the dictionary to mean 'having fine personal qualities and high moral principles'.

So in a relationship, if there is no joy then there's probably a lot of pain. It might be the pain of disappointment or embarrassment at your partner's behaviour, or pain at the lack of communication and understanding between you. Or maybe the love isn't there, or the sex is poor. These things are so often the painful truth about relationships yet often we don't take action.

First we need to be reasonably confident that the person we are with really is right for us, and second, we must treat relationships like a continual journey of progress rather than perfection, and not allow it to become a downward spiral. With these two points, successful relationships are just like successful recoveries – we have to choose a higher power and life-partner that is right for us (to bring us joy), and we must avoid the retrogressive groove of a bad recovery and a bad relationship (which would lead to pain).

Fantasy – Reality

These two words are an interesting test of humility, but that's not immediately obvious – let me explain. Fantasy is a dangerous thing that is so easy to indulge in. When we're drinking, as well as obsessing over booze and filling our heads with resentment and rebellion, we can also indulge in a serious bit of fantasy. The conquest of the perfect sex-bomb or cruising around the Med in a super-yacht (one of my favourites) seem quite benign, but like other problems, they can block us off from our higher power, and recovery.

Reducing those flights of fancy and moving to a state of reality takes significant work on our inventory, and strangely, more in established recovery than early recovery. The problem is, in later recovery, when we are getting everything back together, we start to believe we can now have some of those fantasies. Other defects can keep us blocked off from reality too – pride being the obvious one. When we alcoholics act with pride we tend to actively refuse the reality about something. Finding reality then becomes part of our plan. What is sensibly achievable within our lives, say with a job or where we live? One of the areas where we can seriously loose reality is with relationships, where two people with the heightened emotions of romance, plus a sex-drive, will struggle to keep it real. If we go along for a while in recovery with a good plan and then find a new partner, we can quickly throw away our own plan and come up with new schemes such as spending lots of money together (fancy holidays) or rushing into a serious commitment.

But there's an opposite side to this, and it's the plan we can achieve safely as long as we do it right. I, for one, do want fancy holidays and a great marriage but I have to work in a sensible way to build the foundations for that. That's the reality required.

I suppose one of the purposes of this book is to help us all to bring some reality to relationships. Our default setting with relationships is fantasy, particularly with the personality of an alcoholic, so we need to look hard to find achievable reality.

Sloth – Action

We always say recovery is a program of action. There is the initial effort to get to meetings and to fight the obsession of alcohol. Perhaps we start doing the tea at meetings so that we take some small responsibility for others. Then we choose a sponsor and start the steps. The real action then comes when we get to step 4 onwards. Hard work is required to really change the habits of our character defects – time and time again our faults creep back in and we have to find the stamina to keep pushing them away.

So we should step back and examine our daily lives for the problem of sloth. When I look at myself, I do see some laziness and procrastination. An extra coffee break, a skim through Facebook, a rest on a deck chair in the garden or an afternoon snooze. I justify it by saying I deserve it – or even, get this, it's part of my step eleven. Now we are all different, and balance is required. Sometimes I'm genuinely a bit knackered and forty winks can refresh me. Of course it also depends on the complexity of our lives. If we've chosen a single life and maybe work part-time, we can afford to take it easy. If we've got a big mortgage and three kids, then not so much.

Action should be an attitude. Always put more than enough effort into your recovery, and do it properly and deeply – all the steps and big inventory lists. And sponsor people. If you've got more free time, do more service for AA such as intergroup. Do the bridge to normal living stuff; decorate your house, plan a charity walk, save up for a tour of India. Be creative, take up art, try writing or start a little business. Get into the swing of this, because you'll need it for a successful relationship. Slothful behaviour is not attractive, it's not sexy – period. Oh, and did I say sloth is a big cause of resentment?

You reap what you sow. I can see now that action is the seed of living. We have to build a structure for this though. It's part of the general debate about planning. As we get into recovery we can see how bad we were in the past at getting anything done, so now we start to plan a great life, a life of action, adventure and romance. Seems daft, but that's what I did. I didn't sit around on my arse, I made several big life changes to really improve things and in the end found a partner who is a blast and fills my life with joy. She's not perfect - but there's one thing you cannot stop her doing – every day of her life is full of action.

Unmanageability – Order

Unmanageability of the mind, to me, is just as much a problem for us as alcohol. The second-half of step one says our lives have become unmanageable but people often mistakenly think that means in the past, or up to the point when we stopped drinking. But substitute one word there and I think we are much closer to seeing the truth – our minds have become unmanageable. The word unmanageable is a bit like untidy, or that there's too much to do in a situation and we won't get it all done in time. But it's much worse than that. Our character defects are now ruling us, and they will substitute almost any sensible thought or action with a crazy one. That's the insanity we start to consider in step two and onwards.

To gain order out of this unmanageability, just like any civilised society, we have to start to organise, put infrastructures in place, even put laws in place to stop seriously wrong things running unchecked. We have to be efficient with our time and balance the books. The people need to eat healthy and have some harmless fun. You can see the analogy.

So we must seek some order in our minds. One of the first things I do when I start sponsoring someone is look for the top one or two things that keep occupying their thinking. Here's what I mean. If you start going through some of the steps or inventory work say, an early sponsee will nod and agree, but literally as soon as the meeting finishes, 'bam', their favourite overpowering thoughts come straight back in and they can't even remember what you were talking about. So I try and deal first with that problem, not wait until it appears as one of the many items on their inventory list. For example it might be a particular resentment, or guilt about something specific. I ask them to raise awareness of how those particular thoughts just fly into their mind - and to just try and stop it. I usually suggest they imagine a big red stop sign and a slogan below that reads "STOP – this feeling is not real and it's a waste of time". Later on of course, the sponsee will need to learn about replacing the resentment with something better.

When it comes to building a healthy relationship, perhaps first reflect on how you tackled unmanageability yourself in your early days of recovery. Maybe you got a better job and now you're punctual, polite and effective – and the boss likes you (because of the qualities in you that he can rely on). Perhaps you've improved your routine – you make your bed and wash up your breakfast things before you leave for work, and you prepare a proper evening meal when you get home again. You do your recovery work in an ordered way too, read your daily readings, add a few notes to your inventory list. Now, you are doing things in an ordered way, including a lot of your thinking.

So now all you do is carry that over into your relationship. Keep working on structure that brings order and remove things that are unmanageable.

Unappreciative – Grateful

We talk about gratitude in the rooms. We have gratitude week where we put money in a pot. And our sponsors might suggest we write a gratitude list in the early days, when we have bouts of "poor me". But often we don't go much further than that.

I found we need to look deeper into what is really going on here. We know about the obsession of the mind and how our alcoholism can always try and drag us back to a drink. Maybe the problem is ego and grandiosity, but it's more likely to be resentment, fear, guilt and remorse. And if left untreated these make us restless, irritable and discontent – the discontentment being the poor me feelings. This state can also become an obsession of the mind. You see, our alcoholism wants us to have any negative obsession possible, for our mind to grab onto, and when that can't be resolved, it then want's to make that final jump back to drinking.

For me, my head can still amplify any negatives. When those feelings take a bit of a hold, they 'morf' into thoughts that there is something wrong – something that needs fixing. This exaggerated idea that everything needs to be fixed is bad news and can be a real feature with problems in relationships.

You may have heard the story of the good wolf and bad wolf. The one where the son and father are talking and the son is asking what's the difference between good people and bad people? The story builds up and ends on the idea that we all have a good wolf and bad wolf within us. The son asks which wolf will he turn out like. The father says "you'll turn out like the one you feed". In a way this is the essence of the unappreciative – grateful spectrum.

So our moods and behaviours drift towards the things we spend our time thinking about. Take time to reflect on this and really think about the things that take up a lot of time in your head. If you see that you're spending a lot of time on negative things, or having disturbing feelings, then this needs real work. You're feeding the bad wolf and you're going to be snappy or argumentative, short on patience and tolerance or maybe worse, heading towards depression (and certainly not a nice person to be in a relationship with). So this is where the gratitude list comes in. And work it – feed the good wolf all the time.

Being unappreciative of your partner will cause real damage. You should have lots of genuine gratitude for every aspect of your partner as a human being and the person whom you love, and who is in-love with you. Looks, character, personality, what they do for you, how they care for you. Make them really feel and believe your gratitude. Make sure when you do things for them it's done out of this deep gratitude. This is a big part of love. Tell them your gratitude and love are closely combined.

One particular part of of the unappreciative – gratitude principle is worth a little more discussion. If you were in your relationship when you were drinking and treating your partner badly, their perception of the relationship is probably not good. Remember they will blame you and resent you for quite a while for what you put them through. You just have to keep riding that out. Try not to justify or defend – accept your part in it. Maybe your partner's actions were not as good as they should have been either, but remember what you would have been like to live with – your insanity will have rubbed off onto your partner. The essence of this is that everyone is pretty hurt and damaged because of what has happened and therefore everyones default is to remain very unappreciative of you even as you start to make improvements. Your job is to keep going, put all the work in you can – slowly your higher power will start bringing in some gratitude.

Not to Love – To Love

And so, we come to love itself. I thought for many years that I knew what love was, but really, I didn't. A great part of our journey in both recovery and relationships is learning more about love. I suppose the basic opposites are either not to love, or to love, but it turns out that this is a difficult principle to deal with in a single pair, so I have split it into three.

Hate – Love (as in love thy neighbour)

Hate is a terrible thing. To me it's both a coagulation and amplification of some of the worst human defects – intolerance, pride and greed spring to mind. If left uncontrolled, these faults go through resentment first, then hatred, then sometimes into terrible action.

Our world has been ravaged by hatred for thousands of years – it has been the driver of wars, oppression, racism and countless other crimes. Herein lies an indicator of the spiritual condition of ourselves and those around us. I think that most of us, back in the days when we were drinking, built up some huge resentments against someone, (usually because they were trying to stop us drinking), that turned into hatred. With our raging addiction and rioting self-will, hatred would flare in an ugly fashion. Part of recovery is recognising these darker aspects of our past and doing something about them. We learn about our unmanageability and powerlessness, and we inventory these troubling events, looking to understand the insanity we were suffering from and the damage it caused. Through this work we see how any action, or thinking, based in hatred is so awful – it truly is the worst opposite of any type of love. As we move away from such a condition in ourselves, it's surprising how ugly it looks when we see it in others. For me, I'm now quite cautious of people who say they hate. You hear it quite a lot, muttered under the breath.

One of the central elements of religion is not to hate one another. When we put aside for a moment the issue of faith in a god, we can see that the intent of genuine religion is peace and harmony, without hate. Love thy neighbour is a clever expression because your neighbour is not part of your family and so may be quite different from you, but if you look out for your neighbour and they look out for you, then you're all going to have a much safer community to live in. This is the same as the function of fellowship in recovery, the benefit of a supportive team at the office, or the charity that flows from a great volunteer organisation.

So, the opposite of hate is action to do some of these loving things. To get involved and deliver something. In the fellowship, those of us who get this, start to do service and sponsor others. But in the bigger picture, as we grow, it becomes more than just 'give it away to keep it'. We move out into church or charity work, or start helping selflessly with people in need among our family or friends. Do this and you change. From the selfish alcoholic comes a person who gives out love, administers love to those around him by lowering fear in others, making others safer and suffer less, and have better life-outcomes. I can tell you for sure, do these things for others and you will be loved.

Part of the purpose of this book is to make you a better prospect for someone else as a partner. Well, the change brought about in a person's character by this type of outward giving is palpable, esteemable and very attractive. Replacing the wasteful drunk with someone who gives so much can only come about by deep ego deflation and good humility – and if it's genuine, it always shows.

Childish (Possessive) Love – Adult Love

Possessive love is a childish behaviour. A child who loves her soft toy is incredibly possessive over it. Take a favourite toy away from a young child and you have an instant problem. So it's very possession based, the object of the child's love is the toy; a possession. To covet is another way of describing possessive love, and in the bible it says not to covet a neighbours wife (or is it an ox?).

If this behaviour remains with us into adulthood it can be applied to people, places and things with bad results. Over the past few years I've come to love fine watches and I can feel that childish coveting for them. Hopefully this is relatively harmless, but it's interesting that this particular feeling is still there.

Applying any significant amount of possessive love to other human beings is invariably disastrous. My watches don't complain; they don't mind that I have absolute power over them, but people always do mind. Possessive love of people is directly linked to control of course and if people rebel against our possession of them, we may try to counter that with yet more control.

One of the classic examples of the possessive love problem is usually perpetrated by shallow men. Courting is based on a thinly disguised sexual desire and then if the guy gets the girl, he sees her as a sexual possession and his love for her is like that for a possession. Women can mislead men too, such as wanting more security but not working for it themselves, so this is a form of possessive love also. Gold diggers and sugar daddies are two of the unpleasant terms used for these sorts of people I believe – and there are more of them about than you might think.

We can all see clearly that we need to deal in adult forms of love, much like the love we have learned in the fellowship – we must try and unconditionally love our fellows, care for them and help them in any way we can, regardless of who they are or what their situation is. Strong possessive love has none of this higher spiritual content, so has no place in the lives of those needing to live along spiritual lines. It's a destructive process for us. And for good relationships too, we must work towards love in its mature and responsible forms. It cannot be possessive – or childish.

I mentioned just now unconditional love, but I believe now that adult love should not be totally unconditional. There always has to be a balance and there always has to be a too-far-left or too-far-right judgement call. If you are in a relationship and it's just not rewarding or safe for you then it's not wrong to put that requirement, or condition, on it. It's conditional on the relationship being good for both of you.

You know, this last point is a really hard one to get your head around, even harder to then take action if the love in your relationship is not good enough. But really, how many couples keep going and going, perhaps one is taking advantage of the other, or both are totally miserable – they almost stop living, it gets that bad. I just think that more of us would be happier if we had the courage to really face the truth about the love in our relationships, and take the right action.

Bad In-love – Good In-love

The childish – adult love problem discussed above then leads us to this pair.

Let's go back to the idea that in-love is an instinct. This makes sense to me simply because it can drive our behaviour very forcibly. And so, like any other instinct it can be good, or bad. Just think for a minute what you feel like when you suddenly have that in-love feeling for someone. This probably first happens in our early teens, perhaps someone in our school comes to our attention in a new way. It feels different. Some might argue it's just the sex instinct, and sure it must be connected to that of course, but our thoughts at that point don't really revolve around anything sexual. But why? I think it's because to just be driven by an instinct to reproduce is not the whole part of what's beneficial to human development. In-love drives so many other things which are also vitally important for the wellbeing of the species. Good in-love regulates the sex instinct perhaps – just think how abhorrent it is when we hear news about sexual abuse in all it's forms. Sexual abuse is surely another form of self-will run riot, at an instinctual level, and if most of us were driven by it without any sort of counterbalancing instinct, we'd live in debauched anarchy and wouldn't love people at all.

Let's come back to that point where you're becoming aware that you have feelings for someone. Having those unexpected feelings cause quite significant changes in us. We might get shy or blush in the other person's presence, or try and be funny too much. But the in-love feeling becomes a strong desire to see the other person, spend time with the other person, be romantic with the other person or, not so nice, perhaps control the other person. As alcoholics we have never learned what to do in this situation, and one thing we know in recovery is we have to learn everything properly again – right from scratch. Oh, and one other thing, those desires release endorphins – very dangerous.

When we progress along the path of a relationship a little, the in-love feelings become stronger. And at some point we then usually pluck up the courage to tell the other person earnestly "I love you". And there it seems to stop. What I mean is, we don't build on the responsibility to love the other person properly.

So the strong in-love feeling can distort our behaviour in a bad way. The obvious things we might see are a lack of humility (bravado), poor prioritising, or worse, a drop in our levels of honesty. The in-love declaration between two people becomes a we're-in-love declaration to the world, and that seems to change everything. What we do in our daily lives can change dramatically as we get re-focussed on our new-found relationship. We can for example, abandon our duties to other friends and family, become less diligent at work or reduce our service to the Fellowship. Then comes the problem that the relationship becomes too important to take risks over – in particular for us, that might mean not being honest about who we really are. We are masters at putting up masks and if we are fearful about our character and our past we will be tempted to hide it from our new partner. So maybe now you can see what the left hand end of the bad/good in-love principle might look like. Failure and pain lies here if we stay in this part of the principle.

So when we fall in love, what things can we try and do to practice this principle in a better way? What's at the right hand end of the line? Well the main thing is to make a change in our interpretation of the expression I love you. Rather than it just meaning a declaration of an emotional feeling, how about it means a declaration of intended action? After all, it's always about action. So "I love you" becomes "I will love you – properly, with honour and respect and good actions, when you're unwell or in trouble… and so-on". Sound familiar?

How is it when we get to marriage, that the wedding vows are only thought about then? Or if we're not going to marry, that they are not considered at all. Like it or not, people of religious faith have realised how important these values are, and the wedding vows are central to the service for very good reason. Spend some time as a member of a good active church and see how many are in long-lasting and very loving relationships. Saying vows only once is a bit like reading through the steps once – both are pretty useless if we don't practice them every day.

So I think the right hand end of the good in-love principle is adding to our daily actions those things that we should do for the person we wish to love – and be loved back by. And therein lies another important element of the good in-love principle. It has to be a team effort.

One of the big risks we throw into our lives is falling for someone unsuitable (as our mother's might say). Unsuitable in essence means they won't good-in-love-you. But hopefully with the new found clarity and responsibility we gain from recovery, and perhaps from this book, we can be more objective about who's suitable. This sounds harsh of course but we've probably never been sensibly selective in the past and look where that usually took us. Can we afford to enter into another relationship with someone who won't love us properly, who thinks and operates in the left hand part of this principle? I don't think so. And now that we have more tools, and better understanding, we can assess this and de-risk it.

It's quite easy to spot the defects of a poor in-love attitude. I mentioned control as one but there's jealousy or deeper emotionally undermining tactics too. And you can also step back and look for general good spiritual living in a potential spouse, look right across the board I would suggest and if there are any glaring gaps, you should be cautious. After all, if someone is determined to love you properly, according to a good old set of wedding vows, they're going to be pretty much doing it all anyway in all the other aspects of their life.

Chapter Seven – More On The Topic Of Self

I found that it's only by identifying and working on our principles, that we start to get a proper understanding of self. If we're good inside with self, we'll be good outside, with other people. But that takes a lot more work than you might first think – this is dangerous ground for pride to quickly creep in again. It's very easy to start going around saying "hey I've cracked this self thing you know, I'm well balanced and lovely – you should go out with me". And it's dangerous for you to believe someone else when they lay this chat-up line on you, at least until you have enough understanding of it all to correctly assess if what they are saying is true.

There are many ways in English that we express elements of self. Self-aware, selfish, self-defence, self-indulgent, self-sacrifice, self-centred, self-seeking, self-absorbed, selfless. Here's the point though, we are all defensive, oversensitive or egotistic about self, even how we describe it. If you say to someone they are selfish they are usually deeply offended, if you say to someone they are selfless they feel highly complemented.

In a relationship, I think it's particularly important to break through the barriers of self-defence or self-pity (there's another one), and get to discuss quite literally, our selves (or our selfs?). We have to be so careful when self feels threatened and a partner can subtly threaten it in a great many ways.

Self Deception

We know that our chances of a good recovery revolve around our ability to be honest. This problem is the main target of step five. In essence, we will often be self-deceiving, believing that a certain erroneous attitude or action is a good one, with self-generated reasons to back it up. We create incorrect motives within ourselves by fabricating the wrong evidence in our minds as to why we should or should not do something. This is the core of our character defects in general.

This process of bad evidence can cause a lot of problems in relationships, and vastly more so if you both start doing it. This is an issue for any relationship of course, but for us alcoholics the problem can be much worse. When we get a good sponsor for the first time, one who really starts pushing us, it can be very distressing when they point out a flaw in our thinking but we can't see why what we're doing is wrong (which will always happen). Your own defects are creating incorrect reasons, leading to incorrect assumptions. You're self-justification is wrong – you must replace it with the reality of the facts and the reality of what is needed to replace it (a good principle).

In a way it's like a rite of passage for recovering alcoholics – and a spiritual revelation. To be told half a dozen times by your sponsor, so clearly, where your actions are wrong, is hard. And here you have a critical choice – do you truly cast out all your rebellion, swallow your pride and back down, surrender to the clear direction your sponsor has given you and try with all your heart to stop the fault the next time it's about to occur? Or don't you?

Now, think about this with relationships. If we learn that the only route to recovery success is getting down to that type of deep, responsible action with a sponsor, can it be any different with a partner? I sometimes hear people say that there are a lot of things they share with their sponsor but would never share with their partner. I don't think that's right – it's like there is a rule that I must share with another (one) human being, and then I'm done. I'm not suggesting share things that would harm them or others, but what about all those defects that impact you both today and in the future? What about getting down to the same level of honesty and effort with how you function together and what you can do to keep improving it? Do that, and I think you'll find you won't have many things left that you haven't shared.

Other Peoples' Selves

As well as understanding our own selves, we need considerable wisdom about the selves of other people. Let's consider some examples where other peoples' selves can be damaging to us.

Many of us, as we move into a good long-term recovery, get good jobs, and promotion too – we have the skills to take on more responsibility. But beware, as you do move up, you will come into contact with a lot more people driven by out-of-balance self. Strong ambition, greed, self gratification, pride, status, money and power. Not great when you start to feel the effects of that in a work environment. And if you happen to land in an organisation where there isn't good management training, fairness, equal pay, sensible working hours, good teamwork and welfare support, the effects of those out of balance selves will be even worse. Unfairness, lack of proper recognition, being taken advantage of, or even being undermined and bullied become serious issues.

Likewise you will see problematic selves in certain social environments. Competitive activities such as sports spring to mind here, where recovering alcoholics may get involved legitimately as they join back in with life. Again be aware and cautious – often it's good stuff, but sometimes people get distorted in their competitiveness, acting out with jealousy, judgement and unfairness. Then there's schools, where teachers and parents can clash needlessly, again because of selfishly entrenched views or ideas that just don't make sense.

But when it comes to families and relationships, whether in recovery or not, often the elephants in the room are bigotry and judgement, and the power struggles that these two faults bring. When we say we should hand over, or not react, or not judge, that is easy when it's a short term disagreement with someone in a meeting say, but when there's been half a lifetime's worth of it within a family, within a relationship, or within a work environment, then we're in big trouble.

Let's go back to basics with these two problems. Bigotry is quite a fancy word that is not used very often – it's sort of gone out of fashion these days. Simply, it means intolerance towards those who hold different opinions from oneself. It's a prejudice really, except not against race or religion and so perhaps not as obvious. When it's subtle but continuous, it's incredibly damaging. We all get used to seeing politicians arguing opposite opinions on TV, and might occasionally fall out with someone about the player selection for the next big rugby match, but what about the person who is always closed-down and made to feel foolish in the face of an over-opinionated spouse? Ah, we often say someone is over-opinionated, maybe a bit mouthy or over-enthusiastic but that's not really harmful. The harmful part in the problem is the intolerance. The intolerance of bigotry twists the difference of opinion into a disapproval, a sneer, mockery or argument. When it's like this, it's one of the worst forms of bullying. And that's where the next part of the problem comes in – this behaviour goes hand in hand with judgement. If we cross someone who is a bigot, there is then swift judgement on their part. They might put us down directly, say they are disappointed or more subtly suggesting we are making them angry, or hurting them. Or the judgement can be shared by the bigot with other people – trying to get other people to take their side and collectively disagree with your opinion. The bullying part is of course rooted in control and power, particularly in close relationships. And if we are caught in this cycle with a family member or partner, it can be a continuous loop where we are hurt, or constantly defending ourselves, or avoiding discussions and just operating on a level of almost permanent people-pleasing in order to keep the peace.

Now sometimes we might have to work within this loop, if say we have a cantankerous elderly family member who is not going to change. But here, we are talking about personal relationships and I for one feel that if these particular issues cannot be resolved effectively, at depth, then such a relationship is too dangerous for us.

It says in the big book that fear runs through our lives like a corrosive thread – but remember, corrosion eventually breaks things down to a dust – nothing useful is left. And Bill said we have to work to reduce fear as much as possible and learn how to deal with what remains. So we have to be honest about the causes of fear and if it's the behaviour of another person that won't change, then we must face that fact. Deep down, people who judge all the time don't understand how their own self-will is distorted, and I suspect they find it very hard to get to grips with the practice of humility. So in real terms, removing deep bigotry would take a full spiritual programme and probably as much step-work as removing the obsession for alcohol.

Talking of obsessions, there are others that can cause problems for us. For example, materialism, where proper spiritual value is transposed onto possessions such as property, clothes and cars. Gift purchasing and gift giving becomes a self-driven cycle of control, expectation and judgement.

154

As we experience, observe and understand all these forms of self, and their problems, we stand a much better chance of navigating successfully through this new world of sobriety, and of course, back into families and relationships. I didn't realise for a long time that studying how selves behave would finally enable me to decide with clarity and certainty what someone lovely really means.

Dealing with My Own Self

I used to think a lot about myself in terms of my character defects. I'd feel bad or do something wrong and then suddenly remember a line on my step four and the associated replacement principle. Of course, this is the master process that we should always use with any significant problem. But there are many times when I find it more beneficial to take me out-of-self in more imaginative ways, that seem to be quicker and more effective under everyday conditions. There are three ways I do it:

One – The Robot:

A robot can only do the tasks it is programmed to do and it does them without emotion, anxiety or self-judgement. It's only following lines of instructions written into its memory (by its higher power?) and it goes line by line at full speed through the sequence of the software programme. It doesn't stop (procrastinate) or feel hard done by and it always does its task in the same way – neither over-excited about it or depressed at the prospect. So when I have to carry out a laborious task, say in business or around the house, I sometimes 'do the robot'. I push aside emotion for that period of time and go for it. The real beauty of this is that once other people understand and trust what I'm doing, they don't feel sorry for me or worry about me doing a robot task. When my wife needs something doing that she can't do but worries about asking me, I say "don't be concerned, I'm just going to be a robot". So she knows I'm not cross with her about it, or doing it fast to make a protest. And I will do the task again if she asks, still with no bad feelings (I just hope she cooks me a nice dinner at the end of the day).

Two – Standing next to Jesus:

This is a development of several concepts that I picked up from the Fellowship and active church. Bill W wrote of his idea of the path of humility – that grassy path in the sunlight of the spirit which I like so much, and somewhere else I read about imagining I was sat on a beach with St Francis, and what I might ask him. So under certain conditions I suddenly find myself imagining I'm stood next to someone incredibly spiritual, on a sunny grassy path, and asking them something. It might be St Francis or it might be Jesus, I don't really know and that doesn't seem to matter. Usually it's not much more than a short question about what I should do in a certain situation. All I get in return is a reassuring look or a slim smile perhaps with a simple yes or no. It's like when you meet someone holy, like the monks on Caldey Island, who say very little. I remember one monk just saying to a group of us, "don't judge, never judge" as he gazed upon us with peace in his eyes. So I feel that warmth, security and love, and the depth of far more wisdom than I can comprehend, when I ask my question.

Three – The steampunk machine:

I use this one when I feel inundated with lots of things to manage. We all have that unmanageability feeling creep in now and then and I for one start to lose my reason and perspective under such pressure. In these sorts of situations the big question is, do we need to manage – or just monitor? Imagine that you are going to design a big machine. It's complicated, with boilers, pistons, pipes, cogs and all manner of spinning wheels and sliding contraptions. Maybe it's one of those old ocean liners. Now there's lots we need to know about this machine when it's all running at full steam. Are the pressures right, do we have fuel, do we have oil, are things running at the right speed? Now, we could run madly around our ship, checking each part is doing its job right. But not only is that exhausting, we can only be in one place at a time, so whilst we're checking one widget here, something might be going wrong with another widget elsewhere on the ship.

Or, we can be a bit smarter than this. We can design some ways of measuring stuff in our big machine, and with pressure tubes and little spinning shafts we can build ourselves a bank of dials and gauges – genius. So that's my steampunk machine. It's a great big bank of gauges, and it's hot, noisy and oily, hissing and whirring with activity. Except of course the gauges are not boiler temperatures or propeller RPM, they are all the parts of my life. But the gauges are grouped too, and there are big ones and little ones. And each one has a needle and as the needle moves around from left to right like the speedometer in a car, it passes from green, to amber and then to red. And clearly green is good and red is bad. The groups of gauges might be 'my recovery', 'my relationship' and 'my job' and in each group there is one big master gauge which shows the overall condition of that section. And then sub-dials might indicate the smaller things about the group such as 'the boss is being a twat again' gauge in the section for my job.

How it works is simple. Sometimes I'll be out on a quiet walk say, and I feel upset about something that's going on, and there's its little gauge, needle teetering on the verge of red. But if I look across the whole panel I can see if the big gauges are still in the green. Is my job still okay despite the problems with the boss? If I stand back and look at all the other job gauges – money is in the green, my overall performance at my job is in the green, co-workers also in the green, days off left for holidays just in the amber but that's okay, so it's just the boss in the red. But does that push my overall job gauge into the red? No it doesn't. It's only just up a little towards amber and all I need to do is be patient and the boss will calm down. Some of the big gauges are more important than others too. If the master job gauge goes up into the red, and I have to move on, then does it affect my recovery gauge? Well yes, it might tip it into amber for a while because I'm a bit stressed and fearful, we all have bills to pay, but I can spend more time reading and meditating now I'm between jobs, ensuring those other recovery gauges stay well into the green – and keep recovery in the green overall. And of course, if some of those important systems in my steampunk machine start to get into trouble and quite a few gauges are edging up into the red then I need to take maintenance action – and my bank of dials shows me clearly where I need to get to work.

Becoming Selfless

To end this chapter I thought I would pose the question of how we might become truly selfless. It's a funny thing to consider if you think about it. Surely if we are 100% rid of self there would be nothing left of us. Then you hear of people being praised for selfless acts. So again using the military example, what about real hero's? Those men and women who are awarded the Victoria Cross or Medal of Honour for conspicuous bravery in the presence of the enemy? Surely that must be real selflessness?

So maybe that's how it should work. Selflessness is not fading to zero, it's stepping up in the face of things that are wrong or really might hurt us. And not just by chance; a hero weighs up the situation, sees clearly what the danger is then makes a plan to go in front of that danger to achieve the objective, or save lives. But the hero also calculates that the chances for their own survival is low. That's the bravery – knowing the danger, but taking the action anyway.

So when we examine ourselves, how much selflessness do we find that's like the bravery of the hero? We sense danger a lot of the time, feel hurt a lot of the time, but we also know what action is required - for sobriety and good relationships. And in our case a lot of the hurt and fear is not real anyway, it's imagined.

Chapter Eight – Practical Matters

There are a huge number of practical issues to all aspects of life. When we're drinking, we rarely concern ourselves with anything practical. When we get into recovery we might at first not do very much to establish practical foundations. Yet at some point we will have to – practical matters can be the root of a lot of unmanageability. Also, whilst most practical considerations relate to the security instinct there are additional, important practical matters that support the in-love and sex instincts.

Let's look at unmanageability first. Because practicalities can cause unmanageability, we have to deal with them by using the recovery toolset in just the same way that we do with everything else in our lives. I have found that if you don't use this approach you can get buried under the stress of trying to do too much, you can procrastinate and not get things done, or do the wrong things for the wrong reasons. Character defects can creep in, such as becoming obsessive about organising, becoming a hoarder or trying too much to control other people's surroundings. The Big Book shows us an example of the problem in the chapter for the family afterwards, where the recovering father buries himself in work because of the guilt of past financial trouble.

Another way of looking at it is from the spiritual/mental/physical angle. Our relationship with the physical world seems like it comes third in our priorities, and for some in recovery who perhaps choose a simple, insular life, that may be true. But if you have, or want a family and friends, have a job and want a good relationship, you're going to have to do a lot of practical stuff – you will literally have to build a physical bridge back to normal living.

Now hold your nerve here because this sort of talk can sound daunting to us alcoholics. We have to go slow, keep it in the day and ask for help. We must check our decision making processes with sponsors – we're just as bad at choosing the right apartment as we are the right way to tackle resentments. We need help with budgeting our money, at least until we get the hang of it. That needs planning, which is another alien concept (except for the odd bit of bad planning such as expensive boozy holidays). Planning can trouble us greatly because that's 'projecting into the future' so we have to be careful to use our mindfulness processes (step 11) so as not to overdo it. You will need to practice gentle planning, without too much control or overly projecting outcomes.

The first issues that stand out at this point are income and living arrangements. How do you get your money? If you're on benefits or your family is supporting you then times are going to be tight for a while. You might be paying-off debt too. When it comes to choosing a job, make sure you go through it all very carefully with your sponsor.

The same goes with your living arrangements. You might need to just clean up your place, and pay some bills. Or you might need to move and get settled into somewhere new. If your'e staying in a family home then contribute to its upkeep in a practical way by taking your fair share of the load. But keep an eye on your humility and pride – make sure you're doing the right amount of the right things and watch out for bad decision-making or being taken advantage of. Again discuss your plans and options with your sponsor because that can help you keep on track without burning yourself up about it.

The practical issue I'm going to raise in detail first though, is other people's drinking.

A Relationship With Someone Who Drinks

First off, if your parter is anything more than a light social drinker, I think you're really going to struggle making the relationship work, or indeed, safe. I know this from personal experience.

We all know that at the core of things, our recovery must come first and the power of alcohol must be kept at arms-length. If a partner is drinking regularly and/or heavily, the risk to your sobriety is high. And not just because of the obvious presence of the drink – someone who is drinking regularly is going to be problematic for you, even if their behaviour is considered by them and others to be acceptable. To me now, daily living with people drinking around me just seems an alien, distorted thing, one that has too many risks and too many memories.

But if you need, for good reason, to stay in a relationship with a parter who does drink alcohol, you are probably going to need a 'Partner's Careful Drinking Plan', worked out and agreed between you. This might seem tough at first, but it may be a way for you to both manage safely. Central to the plan should be that your partner absolutely never want's you to take a drink. Your partner must respect that you are an alcoholic, the danger of the first drink for you, and that your recovery comes first. If you are out together, your partner should keep a watch out for other people who might try forcing alcohol on you. One thing that happens at parties is people can get very negative about you not drinking, and whilst they might give up on trying to get you to have a drink, they start pressurising your partner to drink more, saying that *your* not drinking should not be spoiling *their* fun. So you need a clear strategy with your partner in these situations

– anything less will almost certainly become a serious problem for you both.

At large functions, like weddings, the other problem is often the disco and dancing situation. It's daunting if someone tries to drag us onto the dance floor. Discos remind us of dancing drunk, and we're very self conscious when we're sober. But one thing I've found helped me with this was going to AA conventions. In the safety of a convention we can go to the party in the evening with our fellows in an environment of total understanding - and practice sober socialising. We can also break some of those demons and get up on the dance floor – it seems as if our bodies just won't move to the music and our dancing just looks terrible. Some recovery buddies and I once joked that the next time we went to a convention we'd get T shirts made up with the slogan 'It's not me doing this – God's moving my legs in mysterious ways'.

Flirting and Fancying People

Flirting and fancying people are basic instinctual urges, so we have to be wary of them. Firstly, those instincts have some similarities to alcohol; people often don't use them responsibly, they can bolster over-inflated egos and they can be very addictive. They can lead us to make bad decisions and bring lots of trouble our way. And furthermore, because we have sexual needs, desires for relationships and insecurities that just love some fawning sympathy, we can be controlled far too easily by other people's flirting. Particularly if they're cute.

And when I say cute, you can instantly imagine a little bit of that attraction hit, and it's fast. How quickly have you blushed or lost your words when you've had a surprise encounter with someone you've though was unfeasibly hot? And the flirt/fancy issue can pose risks to long term relationships – it's surely one of the main culprits for creating feelings of jealousy. I'm sure we've either done, or seen others do, the drunk flirting at the bar with someone else, whilst the partners have been there, to then be confronted by the partner with lots of jealousy and resentment.

But also there's a good side to it. Nice flirting at the start of a potentially genuine relationship is a lovely part of our human existence, and flirting and fancying a long-term partner maintains the excitement and sense of being desired. A relationship that loses all the flirting could become deficient in its sense of purpose and value.

Dating

Let's start this off by first looking at where dating tales place. We can show an interest in someone and start flirting anywhere we meet people, but it tends to happen mostly in bars and nightclubs, our places of work, at sports or activity groups, in the fellowship or through online dating. Two of these are problematic.

First, pubs and night clubs – well, for all the obvious reasons these really are not suitable places for us, but it's worth reminding ourselves of the basics of dating in this environment as a sort of what not to do. At a pub or party we would immediately start the process based on how someone looks, dresses or dances perhaps. Are they cool, do they look sexy, do you fancy them? Alcohol levels are up and inhibitions are down and it seems like a lot of fun. We all have a lot of memories of such times and for us the outcome of these follies are usually disastrous. Your ego takes over, the sex instinct runs riot and there's no way you're going to discriminate properly if the other person isn't suitable. If it's a bad match you might be lucky and realise your mistake in a day or so. Yet from these poor starts many people carry on with bad relationships for years.

PRACTICAL MATTERS

The other problem is online dating. I'm not saying it can't work, we just have to look at the issues and be cautious. There might be reasons why you have limited opportunities to meet people, such as living in remote rural areas, so online dating could be useful. I did try online dating myself many years ago – I think a lot of people in recovery do give it a go. Various problems soon occur with it though. Firstly I'm sure a large number of people online are drunk a lot of the time. I used to get crazy late-night messages from women whom I'm guessing had probably just got in from the pub. Sometimes it was gibberish, and sometimes it verged on pornographic. Another thing is some people online are totally shallow or distorted, just looking for someone with movie-star looks or a big house. And for us, the temptation is not to be honest about ourselves; indeed, in our online description we're surely not going to post the details of our troubled past. So if you did strike up a deeper connection with someone who doesn't know you at all, you're going to have to tell them pretty quickly a bit about your journey, your need for sobriety and so-on. My suggestion would be to discuss this with a phone call before you meet up. If the response is considerate and understanding then you can be quietly optimistic and move things forward slowly. And when you do meet up, you should expect to get questioned about it. Be honest in broad brush strokes is my suggestion; it's not an AA share and definitely don't do a drinkalogue. Take your time and use the principle of attraction rather than promotion. Go on a few dates and just keep it simple, let the other person see you're okay. In these early discussions, you're going to have to clarify your ground rules too, and whilst some people might find your requirements restrictive, some may actually find it a positive aspect. But if you feel your date is not going to embrace your sober living, don't go forward with the relationship.

Meeting people at your place of work, or at sports and activities clubs, has the advantage that you will probably know each other quite well before a date is on the cards. You will have summed each other up in terms of your work ethics or dedication to a sport. You will also probably have assessed each other's character, sense of humour, interests and lifestyle preferences. Now, just look at this list a minute, and see how different it is from our earlier night club assessment criteria. First, it looks boring, people would say that's no fun. But these are the things that are much more important to your wellbeing than someone's moves on the dance floor. Do it this way round and you can make safe progress and get to the smooching later. Do it the other way round and you might as well drive fast through fog.

Then when it comes to meeting people in the fellowship (or church), we have the additional benefit of a common spiritual foundation and probably quite a lot of deep knowledge about each other's journey. All the shares, the service together and perhaps trips away to conventions will allow us to build up a good understanding of each other, and start the bonding process. On a practical note I would make two suggestions; make sure you do the bulk of your dating away from the fellowship and make sure you do some of your meetings without each other. Oh, and when I started dating Kathryn, I found myself on the receiving end of some rather unpleasant reactions from a few people in the fellowship, and I discovered this was the same experience for just about all fellowship couples. Again to me, this is further evidence that we all need to do so much more in this area.

For alcoholics, dating is a risky business full of potential unmanageability. I remember Bill W wrote for Grapevine how he learned that he had to cut himself off from dependancy on outcomes, and when you find the real possibility of a new romantic venture, oh boy, you suddenly become very dependant on it – those instincts will make sure you are. It's the early days where the bulk of the risk lies. So, the first thing is perhaps just to be aware. The problem is, we are in a strange state – both in an attacking mode and a defensive mode – we press forward to get something we want, to the design we want (the new relationship), but we don't want to be trapped or put at risk. And some people are more inclined to be attacking, making the new person in their sights a conquest, and some more defensive, making the pursuit by a suitor a high-threat-level event. Now this is a blunt view but you know what I mean, so when you soften this with the kindness, care and good behaviour that we should have, we can make progress.

But at this time there are some important practical matters to consider. Keep going to your meetings and see your sponsor regularly. Make sure you don't start cancelling fellowship commitments for the chance of a hot date. Don't make any decisions that go too large at the start – things like grandiose holidays or expensive presents don't achieve anything useful at this stage. Indeed, keeping it right-sized demonstrates better qualities in you. And don't make any big changes that your sponsor wouldn't agree with, things like moving house or changing jobs. The key is to remember that neither of you are behaving normally at this stage, so neither of you are really seeing the other in their true light.

Changing Practical Habits

After a couple of years into recovery, I started to do more business trips again. I needed to work extra-hard to keep safe from picking up a drink at these times. Business dinners were occasionally necessary, but the bigger concern was traveling – airports and flights were a constant stream of drinking opportunities. When I used to go to an airport, I was desperate to get through security quickly and make my way to a bar. I'd often check in early – after all, this was a good drinkin' opportunity, with a lovely aircraft seat waiting for me to sleep it off later. But what to do when I had to travel sober? Well actually, I did something that taught me a few important lessons. At airports I started wandering around the duty free perfume stores. My sponsor at the time had taught me about looking after myself physically, dressing better and so-on (more of that later), and I had at some point purchased a bottle or two of cheap shopping-mall cologne. Well, at airports they have the high-end perfume brands, French, a lot of them, with many good scents that smelled very different to anything I had tried before. I would test one or two, then Google about them on my phone whilst having a coffee. And I smiled to myself a few times whilst doing that – how ironic that I had replaced bottles of spirit with, well, bottles of spirit. But also in a real practical way – I had replaced a dangerous process with a much safer one.

One thing I didn't realise at first was this was also about trying to become more attractive to the opposite sex. Booze, although sometimes portrayed as being sexy, really is not, but perfume, well that's pretty much what it's designed for. I also found perfumes that were peaceful and spiritual in nature, that connected me to lovely memories such as my grandfather's garden. These perfumes started to raise my awareness of things I had forgotten about when I was drinking.

After a while, the whole nice clothes, perfume and watches thing went a bit deeper. I think I already said I had become attracted to quality watches, something at first I thought was very selfish, indulgent and totally unnecessary. But enjoying nice physical things is important. I found it's a connection to creativity and human endeavour. And here's the rub, look around and see how many happy, well adjusted folk do have nice clothes, a nice watch and smell good. The answer is of course, a lot of people, and I didn't realise at first, it's normal. Provided it's done in balance, it's an important part of self. It's a little bit of self-esteem and a little bit of the sex instinct and it shows that you take care about your appearance and probably other things in your life too. And I promise you this, do a bit of preening and people around you will react more positively to you, the opposite sex will be more interested in you. Bill W said in the Big Book, about reaching a spiritual experience, "I had arrived", well let's make it look like you've arrived. A recovering alcoholic spouting the good words of sobriety but still wearing his or her scruffy old stuff is not sexy - remember part of this is, literally, attraction rather than promotion.

Shopping and Tidying Yourself Up

The just for today card says 'I will look as well as I can, dress becomingly...' In early sobriety I started shopping trips with one of my brothers. We would go to quality clothes shops and buy a couple of nice shirts. Nothing crazy expensive but something we would budget a little for. Then trousers and shoes. And by stylish stuff I don't mean sportswear or combats, but something in fashion and cool for our age.

When you go shopping, go with a recovery buddy, talk about it and have a laugh, but also be serious about it. And men, don't go out shopping dressed scruffy; scrub-up and dress best you can. The reason – so you can, with confidence, politely go up to a sales woman in a store and ask her advice. She will then happily go around and help you pick out a few things to try – in fact you might be surprised at the lovely reaction you get from women when you do it like this. Why? Because you're starting to practice that little bit of outward self esteem, in a gentlemanly manner, and women respond positively to it. Most women are of course pretty good at shopping, going around finding the latest fashion. But you will also occasionally see a smart, debonair businessman doing the same, either buying for himself or maybe his lovely wife. What message does this give out? Well, that he's probably thoughtful, generous and fun to be with – a good mate to the lucky woman he's about to go meet for coffee and surprise with a small gift. It's normal, attractive, romantic – and what we should be aiming for.

Some women in recovery don't do this stuff very well either. But it's not because they don't know how to, they just seemed to have given up on it, and themselves. So for both men and women we need to find a bit of motivation in order to smarten up. It's the same old thing – take action.

Physical Maintenance

We need to go back to basics with ourselves physically. Our bodies. We only have one body whilst on this planet and we haven't done a very good job of looking after it so far. First of all, it should be a survival thing. Being healthy is better for survival. But in this book we're also talking about dating, kissing, shagging; the whole nine yards. You really are going to do better at that sort of stuff if you're in better shape.

So a big part of this is lifestyle and fitness. Now let's not insult each other's intelligence about food. If, having survived alcoholism and found recovery, we can't correctly identify and follow healthy eating habits, even if that takes a twelve-step programme too, then I can't see how we can be effective with much of the other stuff in this book. We're talking about being active and romantic, a sort of 'sweep her off her feet' type of lifestyle and that takes some fitness and stamina. It's not sexy sitting on the couch after a half-hours walk, sweating and complaining.

So what should we really do? We start by taking a good honest look at ourselves physically. We do it in every other aspect of our lives, so why not our bodies and lifestyle also? Remember there's another doctor's opinion out there that says significant improvements in lifestyle and fitness will bring significant improvements in weight, motivation, sleep, libido, your smell, deportment, your skin, credibility, immune system, attractiveness and many more. Okay, a doctor won't give you a list quite like that, but that is the reality.

You hear people say "join a gym". Just do that and you're almost certain to fail. We have to go about this in the same way as any other part of recovery – change by replacement, progress not perfection and avoiding contempt prior to investigation. We need to see and feel the results from the action. And those results are not body building medals or a modelling contract with Chanel. They are spiritual.

Faith forms part of this also. Think back to our drinking days, when we did almost nothing physical for a long time. We had lost a great deal of fitness and strength, so doing things now hurts and wears us out. A little bit day by day will slowly improve things, but keep a vision in your mind of the long-term aims – going down a dress size, looking smart in a suit, sleeping better.

And I promise you, where the Just For Today card says 'as you give to the world so the world will give to you', second to getting sober, getting fitter is the next big giver to your life. Interesting actually that word, fit. We tend to mainly think of the word fit regarding physical fitness. But what about that girl who works in the bank, "wow, she's fit", what about in the military when a pilot is declared "fit for combat" and what about in engineering when a piece of machinery is declared "fit for purpose"? It means we can do all the things we were designed to do, do it under pressure, and look sexy whilst doing it. How do I know this is true? Well, from my own experience of course, but also by really listening to other people's stories. People get into recovery, have relationships, do service, go to church – all bringing great improvement to our lives. But you will NEVER hear a more joyous response than someone who says they have slowly gained fitness, transformed their physical wellbeing, who feels more attractive and desirable. This is the person who enters a meeting and says things like, "I've got to know someone great in Ramblers and we're talking about a holiday together in Patagonia". Do you see? This is life. And you can have it. Ask your higher power right now if you can have it, and see the answer that comes back.

So, coming back to the practicalities, where do you start? Maybe first, find other people in your fellowship who are active and join in with them. The groups in West Wales organise regular spiritual retreats to Caldey Island, where they go to services in the Abbey as well as having Fellowship meetings, but also go walking around the Island two or three times a day. There are coastal walks and lots of wildlife to see, lovely photo opportunities, quiet spots to sit on your own, or lovely woodland walks to stroll along with one or two other fellows, gently sharing experience, strength and hope.

Go to conventions and have trips out. Ha, have to tell you about my brother Dave. One convention on the Isle of Wight, he decided to bring power kites with him and we all went down to a windy beach to fly them. His demonstration of how a big kite could quite literally pick you up off the ground went somewhat wrong when it lifted him about ten feet in the air and then dropped him on his shoulder. Yep, he had to have surgery on that sometime later, but his words were, "damn, broke my shoulder – but hey, livin' the dream".

One activity you hear discussed occasionally is yoga. One of my close recovery buddies finds yoga very good for fitness and strength and she says it helps hugely with her energy levels, how she sleeps and how she feels about herself. She has also found that the meditation and relaxation side of yoga fits in well with her step eleven processes. So if that sort of thing appeals to you then it's definitely worth a try. And it's another good way of meeting new people.

How we look after ourselves is a reflection of our overall levels of honesty and responsibility. Keeping fit and living healthily recognises the truth that these things are important and when you're in a relationship, or want to be in a relationship, being responsible in this department will make you a much more attractive proposition. The maintenance of your fitness also supports the social and security instinct of the other person. If you're fitter, you can be more active together, you can mix it up with the types of day's out you have. Yes, sometimes it's dinner and a show, but sometimes it should be a yomp across the moors.

A lack of fitness causes other problems too. What if the other person identifies your inactivity as sloth? They might wonder why you can't see the defect and change it in order to bring the romance alive, make them feel more sexy towards you even. This can then mean their own instincts towards you start to become less positive. For example, security – what if he/she gets ill and can't work? Social – I'm not going to have much of a social life with this person. Sex – well as I've implied, sloth is not sexy. And in-love – "I might have some in-love feelings for this person now, but is that going to last?" We have to remember that the sex instinct is not just about having sex, it's also about the genetic quality of the potential sex partner for reproduction. And whilst you might not be planning to have kids, it doesn't mean this part of the instinct won't be having an effect. It doesn't go well if you're not assessed as reasonable reproduction material by friends and family either. Now sure, this all sounds rather neanderthal, I deliberately wrote it that way. Most of us, as higher-thinking beings, can balance these things out with lots of other value judgements, but I'm just saying that if you are looking to make changes in your life including your physical wellbeing, then it's likely that these things will improve your relationship prospects (not to mention your longevity, employment opportunities and so-on).

Okay, onto something a bit different. And this might seem quite comical or embarrassing, but don't underestimate it. Hands up who knows what a Brazilian is? Or more precisely, a Brazilian wax? No? I suggest you Google it. The point is, intimate personal grooming is important if you want to make a positive impression when the time comes. Now, women are pretty good with legs, underarms and bikini lines – it's a permanent part of modern life for them. Women are comfortable with all the epilators and potions required for the job and if they want to take things a bit further with a razor, or a visit to a beauty clinic, then that's well within their comfort zone. But men; not so much.

Now guys, the truth is that if you resemble a hairy bear from top to toe, it's likely to put a lot of girls (or guys) off. A nice haircut, (and if you're thin on top, no combovers) and a well trimmed beard or a nice clean shave. You can get away with stubble on the second day of a dirty weekend. Get a nasal/ear hair trimmer and use it regularly. Underarms – trimmed short. Chest hair trimmed or shaven depending on what you think best suits. And down there in the trouser department? Well trimmed, as a minimum, is required at all times, but don't underestimate the benefits of 'going clean'. Now many guys initially freak out at all this. Some may think it's very girly and threatens their masculinity. Girls want to be soft and smooth themselves and they might just like you being soft and smooth too. Don't forget contempt prior to investigation because the real answer here is, chaps, find out what your girl likes. Start off from the well trimmed standard and as you explore your sexuality together, make some changes – you may find that playing on a totally clean field floats both your boats. [By the way, I'd like bonus points here for managing to avoid all the puns about not beating about the bush, going balls-out etc].

I mentioned earlier, going shopping for clothes and the fun of nice fragrances – you can add these to your physical maintenance plans too. But there is another major element to tackle; what about living arrangements? I'm not going to go through a list here, it's quite simple to get a good idea of what's required. Just imagine you meet someone new and you suddenly have an unexpected opportunity to invite them back to your place. What will they find when they get there?

Now let's go back to recovery thinking here for a minute because I can hear you all shouting this is vanity and pride, and that people should take us as they find us. Find us? Just think for a minute how people would have found us when we were drinking. Practically unconscious most of the time, pale, smelly, dressed in dirty clothes and sleeping in bedding that hadn't been washed for goodness knows how long. You've got to open your eyes here because that behaviour stays with many of us into recovery. I put it to you that it's more sober to be healthy, clean and tidy with a clean apartment and have some nice suits for work. Oh, here's an interesting point about work. Bill W said that most alcoholics have a higher than average earning potential. Well the prospects get even better if you dress well there. And that feeds back into you being a better relationship candidate because you have a smart job (security instinct).

Smoking

Many of us smoked in our drinking days and we carried on smoking into recovery. We find that the struggle not to pick up a drink seems lessened if we can smoke a cigarette instead. I get that – I did it. In fact, in my early months when I had my first apartment after leaving the family home, I went through a short phase of pretty much chain-smoking even though I hadn't smoked much before. I was very aware of the effect of the nicotine as I smoked, but it also felt like a rebellion, in the same way as in my drinking days I would storm off to the pub when someone said I shouldn't have a drink. But later, I challenged myself to change with cigarettes, to defeat both the rebellion process and the need for the nicotine hit. I found in the end that I had not had a true spiritual awakening until I had come to rely completely on my higher power, for all my needs. Using a cigarette to make me feel better in any way was a deficiency in that regard.

Smoking is also smelly, expensive and very bad for our health. So there's three more reasons not to smoke. Honestly, the money aspect and the risk to health over time are things a relationship should not have to contend with.

Keeping House

When we consider the possibility of building a deeper relationship, the situation of our domestic arrangements should be looked at as part of that work. As we build up our knowledge of the instincts, man-brain/woman-brain and the amount of responsibility required to make a relationship work, we can soon see that how we structure our domestic arrangements is going to be important.

Let's think about the concept of home. We may remember our childhood home life being either good or bad. And some of us have experienced the breakup of family homes as adults and parents. Home is a big backdrop in the wreckage of our pasts. So we need to find a new concept of home. We can start to see it when we look into our hearts and find a connection to our higher power. A place of love, a place of peace, and a place of care and support. A place of safety for a partner.

The sense of spiritual and instinctual safety is one of the main threads through this whole book – if you don't provide that to a partner then a relationship is never going to be healthy. But there are practical elements to this concept too. The security instinct could cover a range of things such as do you own or rent the place where you live? If you're renting is the landlord good? Is the rent you're paying reasonable? If there are problems here, it will add stress to your and your partner's security instinct. Is your home actually homely? Is it decorated nicely and do you have nice furniture, bedding and a clean and tidy kitchen and bathroom? We need to include these things in our plans. Work out if the house or apartment where we live is good enough and if not, plan how we are going to pay for slow improvements. We might need to move house and start fresh in order to build up a good base. It's not hard to see the security instinct things that matter when we do this. Just remember, it will tick a big box in someone else's security instinct too.

And when it comes to the social instinct, is your home a nice place for your you and partner to sit and chat? Place a nice big sofa in front of a good TV, where you can watch movies and snuggle. Can you bring friends round for coffee? And when it comes to some of the little things, like coffee, get a good espresso machine – don't keep serving cheap instant, it's horrible. Buy nice towels, nice soap, keep fresh salad in the fridge. And how about your cooking skills? Both the security and social instincts can be considerably supported by a homely environment with wholesome cooking. Isn't it funny, how as recovering alcoholics struggling to find peace and love we don't think of something as simple and basic as cooking. But buying and preparing good food with quality ingredients is a discipline and a service to ourselves and others around us. It's a real reflection of how far we have come, and what we think is important in life, in small detail. And other people notice.

Chapter Nine – Sex

What a strange thing is the topic of sex. Without it, life on Earth would not exist as we know it (think there's a Star Trek line in there). The most basic process of evolution is the way our genetic codes change, driven by natural selection. That change is then taken forward through the process of reproduction. Plants and animals strive to be better, then pass that improvement on to the next generation. And this creates the sex instinct and sexual competition. Whether that's deer rutting, peacocks displaying their tail feathers or flowers with evocative scents, these are all competitive sexual processes designed to bring about change. And we humans evolve, strut and preen in order to pass on that change just like most other creatures. We seek our mates for this reason.

As recovering alcoholics who want a relationship, we start to rejoin the world of reproductive competition. We learn for the first time about the real risks and rewards of life and what we have to do to become better than we were before. We learn to love our fellows, our families and our partners. If we are involved with an in-love relationship that has a sexual element to it, then surely we need to learn something about sex too. But how often do you speak in meetings, or to your sponsor about sex? If you do at all, I bet it's not at any great depth. And how often do you properly discuss the topic with a partner?

Many people are very fickle about sex and their sexual desires. It's all clouded with fears about our sexual performance, personal image or social or religious dogma that sex is in someway bad. Many things can go wrong with sex. For example because people desire the pleasure of sex, it can be used as a bargaining tool, or if sex is not satisfying in a relationship, it can build serious resentment. So how crazy to expect things to work well in a relationship if sexual matters are not in good order. That's like expecting someone to have strong sobriety with a badly out of shape ego.

Any problems in the sex department are going to have a direct impact on us in just the same way as any other untreated issue. Problems that we have not sought to identify, then replace with the alternate good behaviour will always catch us out. If we look at it from a twelve step viewpoint, where we diligently analyse our past drinking, our dishonesty, lack of responsibility, inflated egos and so-on, we get to sex and usually skim over the subject, just talking of how we might have cheated, or perhaps withheld sex to manipulate someone. But we don't talk about lust or passion, sexual exploration or fear around past sexual problems. To make matters worse, we often hear in meetings people bragging inappropriately about past sexual exploits – so it seems unsafe for most of us to express ourselves in this area. Surely we can do better?

A Dumb Society

Society really messes-up with its attitudes towards sex. Sexual stigma starts young. Girls are told by their mothers that boys are stupid and only want one thing (sex). Boys are dragged into a falsely macho world of male dominated activities. The proper interaction between girls and boys is often denied, and on it goes – you can see for yourself hundreds of examples of damaging sexual distortions. It gets very bad for some people – girls are deeply affected, even damaged (eating disorders) by media and marketing regarding their looks. Boys are told by their fathers to toughen-up and not show emotions because its not manly. And social media is rife with gender bullying.

So we go into adulthood with considerable baggage that is further reinforced as we stumble through bad sexual experiences and poor relationships, reacting to other people with equally poor ideas about sex. We could dwell on all these sexual problems that the world creates, but for us it's like cursing the existence of breweries, it's not for us to argue their existence, but only to properly work a path through it for our own wellbeing.

The Real Sex Problem

This whole sex issue is a difficult thing to describe. The desire for sex is multi-layered and seemingly quite random, odd or even objectionable. The identity of sex itself ranges from strip clubs, porn and promiscuity, to tender love and the start of a new family. As alcoholics we've classically wrecked relationships with out of balance sexual demands, or a total lack of interest. But to get us on the right path we can label all those things as alcoholic behaviour, and make the assumption that they are as illogical as hiding booze or not turning up for work. We learn in recovery that we should replace bad with good. So it seems to me that the big question is, if dysfunctional sexual behaviour is bad what are we aiming to replace it with?

Let's start with some basics. I hear so many people in troubled relationships sneering when the topic of sex comes up – "yuk no, I don't let him/her have much sex – not interested in that any more". You might think it's natural for people to go off sex after two or three years into a relationship. However, I ask people one question about that – would you have lots of sex if you started a new relationship? The answer is usually "well yes, everyone has lots of sex at the start of a new relationship". To me, this suggests that the issue isn't people's physical ability to have sex, or the ability to find the passion to have sex, the problem lies with our proper understanding and use of the sex instinct within a longterm relationship. At the start of a relationship, part of the sex element is surely to validate the proposition. It's the test drive of a new car or the walk around a show home – it all looks and feels great and this is what we want. But if people aren't honest, then there's a risk down the line that you won't get what you've paid for.

So what goes wrong? Well firstly I think most of us blame the wrong thing. We go along with the social premise that it's natural for sex to dwindle but I just don't buy it – I think this is the symptom, not the cause. I think the real problem comes down to two of our standard defects: one is sloth and the other is fear – faults that stop us from doing many great things.

Fear About Sex

Let's start with fear. One element of the fear problem comes from one of our society norms, where the topic of sex is kept very secret. Notice I don't say private, but secret. Ask yourself how many people probably have sexual questions, problems or fantasies that they never discuss with anyone else at all. For example, when discussing a new relationship that a best friend has just started, would you ask them things like, "What sort of sex have you tried and are you on the same wavelength with more adventurous stuff"? Or, "Do you both have great orgasms, have enough sex to satisfy each other, laugh about it, dress up in kinky outfits, do it in the morning, on the beach…?" No. We ask what job they hold, are they helpful with the chores, what's their family like. How many people on a second or third date ask their new partner those sorts of sexual questions? Again the answer is almost certainly, not many. We would start dating and start fumbling about, having sex without discussing it at all. No wonder it's so hard to talk and take action about sex later on, because when we realise that the sex might not be so great, the fear has already set in.

Then we come to the fear that we think we don't perform well enough, don't look cute enough, aren't buff enough or might not be as good at sex as some of the other person's previous partners. It's difficult though – who's going to ask a new partner how well they're doing in bed compared to other people they've slept with? Or perhaps our new partner has quite a demanding sexual appetite and we are fearful of damaging the relationship by saying it's not for us so much – so we are dishonest about it and fearful of the possible consequences. Or it might be the reverse for us – our new partner does not seem as interested in sex as we are.

Part of the problem here is we're strangely fearful about intimacy. At least, some of us are. I served in the merchant navy when I was very young, and was once sent ashore in Tokyo to see a doctor. I arrived at the clinic and was ushered into a large room containing about ten desks, with men and women in white uniforms (the doctors and nurses) plus a patient stood at each table. I was shown to one desk and because I was not able to speak any Japanese, I did a little demonstration of how I had fallen, and pointed to my shoulder and ribs. Next, I was clearly being asked to strip. I glanced around and saw other patients in various states of undress, being prodded by doctors whilst one or two nurses looked intently at the patients bodies too. I then more or less freaked-out as the staff started to try and undress me. My behaviour just didn't make sense to them, nor theirs to me. One thing that stood out as a catalyst to my reactions in those few seconds, was seeing a cute Japanese woman stood at the next table in just her bra and knickers, not looking at all flustered as she being examined in plain view. I later discovered that Japan's society evolved quite differently to most others; through the Edo period (1600–1868), westerners were not allowed onto mainland Japan. So the development of the collective sense of personal space and intimacy in Japan was very different to other societies.

Turning to our western experiences, perhaps we can see back to our own childhood when we were frightened to get changed in the gym or being seen by a doctor of the opposite sex. These things surely build anxiety for the times we are going to get naked with a partner. I was very lucky to have that experience in Tokyo, because it showed me just how deep and invisible the effects from our own particular societies can be. It's the start of the whole sex-fear problem.

Sloth Around Sex

The other main issue is sloth. We tend to think of sloth with regard to our lounging habits and in recovery, when we examine our defects we all find some lazy inaction in our lifestyle. We can see how sloth stops us cleaning house, sorting out our finances, getting ourselves fitter, finding a proper job – or doing the steps. This is the same for people without an obvious addiction because most people still make choices not to do the right thing, choosing instead easy gratification such as shopping, social media, TV, food – rather than keeping fit, healthy and sexy. Here's a thing, have you ever met a friend who had been in a long-term relationship that had recently ended, only to find that they are suddenly fitter, slimmer, better dressed – quite glamorous or handsome again? In essence, after the ending of the last relationship, they have fought off the sloth for a while in order to put themselves back on the market.

But for us this sort of problem is not so difficult to see. We are fortunate that we take inventory and make change, understand the concept of principles and know that we have to give to receive. And it also comes back to the fundamental in-love responsibility. Is it not irresponsible to start the in-love instinct in another person and then allow sloth to creep in later? To present ourselves to the other person as quite sexy and attractive, only to take that away later through inaction? Sounds like a harsh way of putting it but there are many times when this will be the basic truth.

We should expand this out to all our affairs, remembering that the in-love responsibility brings a lot of extra focus on our actions (or inaction). This links up with the complexity problem too, of course, so we must also watch out that we're not trying to do so much organising and impressing, keeping fit and earning good money that we're burning ourselves out. So work together in a relationship to find the right balance for you both. And remember to communicate. It's surprising how the wrong impressions can be formed when we don't explain what's going on – a hard day at work and then the need for some rest in the evening might be seen by a parter as a bit slothful if they don't know what our day has really been like.

But what about sloth in our sex lives? Well a lot of that might be linked to physical sloth generally. If, over a long period of time we're not looking after ourselves and we start getting out of shape, then we might start to feel less confident about intimacy. But it also takes mental effort to get in that place where we feel sexy. We've got to keep the romance going, spring a few surprises, buy a new slinky outfit. Talk about it when you both go into town, then take a look at lingerie together (and men, be subtle – don't go straight for the crotchless panties). On holiday, make sure you keep active as a couple. Go swimming, take long walks – get a tan and the salt in your hair, make sure you smell of sweat and suntan lotion. Then when you get back to your room, have sex in the shower together, then go down to dinner later looking classy and a little bit smug.

Sex Inventories

When we first read about inventories in the Big Book it explains the basic process of splitting up our defects into resentments, fears, harms and sex conduct. But the examples given are just starters of course and when we work with our sponsors we soon end up with a lot more detail. At first, the grosser handicaps are revealed and we learn how to find and apply the opposites using steps six and seven. Doing this starts to bring wisdom about the principles to practice. Later, looking back after say a year or two of inventory taking, we will see that the list has grown. In essence, as we have more life experiences in sobriety, we bump into more of our defects and in turn learn something new from each experience [you know, I wonder about people who say they only did step four once – I think they must be largely unaware of the true power of the process].

But with the sex instinct, I would say that for most people in recovery, the inventorying process stops after that first basic look. But there will be no success unless we apply the same vigorous processes that we require for the other parts of our lives. We must inventory. Do you really want to know why? When I said that, in recovery, we bump into more detailed problems about ourselves as we live life on life's terms, well if you start a relationship you are going to be quite literally bumping your sexuality against another person's sexuality. Are you going to go into that totally unprepared for the emotional, instinctual and even addictive pitfalls that might be awaiting you?

You have to look at this in a similar way to alcohol, but with a different sort of responsibility. Alcohol is temptation in a glass and once we are properly sober we avoid it totally. Sex is also temptation, driven by endorphins that produce excitement and lust, but now we're making plans not to avoid it, but indulge in it more. Remember, our sexual behaviour directly impacts another person at the deepest level, so it's a good idea that we are not behaving alcoholically here. I always come back to responsibility, and that's the nub of it I think. Deep, complete 100% responsibility, with an iron clad guarantee to both your higher power and your partner that you will behave impeccably with the sex instinct.

Being responsible here also means we have to communicate our intent to be responsible. And this is the solution when dealing with the legacy of our past and ensuring a problem-free, loving future. When it comes to difficult sex problems, such as the pain of past partner's infidelities, there are always massive scars. So that means two things: working as hard as we can to get over our own pain around past sex problems, and making sure that we never again hurt anyone with bad sexual behaviour.

So we tentatively start to inventory our sex instinct. I would suggest as well as fears, harms and resentments around sex, we inventory the instinct itself at depth. Here are some ideas:

- How did our sexuality develop in adolescence? Did we fantasise about the butch rugby players or the geeky physics guys, the shapely girls in the gymnastics team or the rather mysterious girls in the orchestra? Did we talk about sex a lot with our friends? Were we shocked at discovering explicit things about sex or were we fascinated? Did we masturbate about our fantasies?
- With adolescent sexual experiences, were they good or not? Did those experiences create any fears (if so, they should be on your inventory). Experiences of premature ejaculation or failure to have orgasms are likely to set up some anxiety, and so too are feelings of being coerced into sex, or coercing someone else, through adolescent pressure (not rape).

- How has sex been in previous relationships? Dull or exciting, too much or too little, were there problems and arguments about sex? Did past partners like your sexuality, or did they accuse you of faults? Look at your side of the street in those cases – are there areas you could have done better? As alcoholics (or alcoholics in waiting) we are likely to have been very selfish regarding our sexual wants.
- Really assess your own sexual desires and taboos. Do you only feel comfortable with under the covers missionary position stuff or do you require sex toys and a bit of bondage? If you are restricted in your appetite, you should find out if that is really you or if you are being held back by fear. A considerate but explorative lover in a future relationship might be an incredibly liberating opportunity.

I should say at this point that if there is anything in your sexual history that is more significant than the ideas above, such as suffering from sexual abuse or having a sex addiction, then consider seeking support from professionals or groups who specialise in those areas.

Combining Two Sex Instincts

So, if we head down the path of an in-depth sex inventory for ourselves, we will surely be better set for a sexual relationship with another human being. All our inventories are there to help our relations with other people, we always new that right from the start. It will improve our spiritual condition because we know within ourselves that we have worked on doing Gods will in this area of our life too – all our bad stock in trade needs replacing with good, to get a proper spiritual result. And the old rules apply when it comes to putting others before ourselves –

operating on a selfish sex instinct is going to create the same failures as any other output of a damaged self will.

But with sex, we're now talking about two people, so how do we work together on this? Well, you could slap a list down on the table at the start of your second date and go for it – but I think you'll end up walking home on your own.

So perhaps you can start by raising the idea of being more responsible and loving about sex, discussing how generally relationships can struggle in this department and that you want to find a way to do things better. This sort of approach is gentle yet clearly indicates that you think it's important. This also gives you a chance to assess how your new parter thinks. Remember that you want a happy, functioning sex life and the other person may have a lot of baggage here. You need to find that out too. This is the start of your joint sex inventory.

If all goes well at this level then you can both start to add more to your understanding of your sexuality together. I don't think people would ever be writing lists here, that's not very sexy, but keep the dialogue going about you increasing knowledge of each other's sexual needs. What you like and dislike, how you can try new things that perhaps you didn't want to do before. The point is to build that level of trust and understanding. This is the basis of the humour and naughtiness, tenderness and sexual ecstasy that eludes so many couples because of poor communication, fear and resentment.

What if you hit a defect? Remember that one of the functions of an inventory is to find defects and then take them forward into the change process. I find some people are very quick to shut down the possibility of change in the sex department but I don't see that it has to be any different from working towards change with anything else. Defects are a block – something is in our character that is blocking us. We say something is blocking us off from having peace of mind or the sunlight of the spirit, so why not satisfying sex? Sex is no different from those other two rewards – it's a revelation when we properly find it as God intended.

But what sort of things might potentially block us off? Well, here are four examples that you might experience.

The first is the possession problem. We know that possessing someone as if they are a piece of property, or a possessive or jealous love, is not a good thing. But I'm not talking about that. The point here is that we will, naturally, have some feelings of wanting to possess a sexual partner – in a good relationship. I think in essence this is based in the defence mechanism that we don't want our partner to have sex with anyone else – for genetic/evolution reasons (as well as the obvious feelings of betrayal and inferiority). We are uncomfortable with that thought and we feel a lot of potential pain that would be brought about if our partner were to have sex with someone else. Usually in a good relationship, both partners feel this about the other, but often keep the feeling secret for fear that expressing it would indicate a lack of trust. It's a primal feeling that we try and bury, only to be sharply reminded of it when we hear of infidelity problems with friends or work colleges (and its always on TV as entertainment?). So we can be fearful, but it is okay to feel it. Share about it between you.

The second is the way we feel about the number of past sexual relationships the other person has had. Or indeed, how many we have had. For alcoholics, this count could include all sorts of crazy past experiences. Drunken one-night stands, multiple short relationships or even using the sex industry (there are many places one can go in this world that have booze and sex available 24/7). When people are in addiction and in financial trouble they may even resort to selling themselves for sex. These things will certainly be on the inventory of some alcoholics. But for others, they won't, so make sure you don't assume any of these things about anybody – it's easy with this instinct to let suspicions run riot. But don't make an issue out of numbers of partners. If you can look back at your journey and genuinely see how the events in your life were driven, what happened and why, and that you no longer want to live like that, then I think that's totally acceptable. If you had phases of high promiscuity, you can't change that. Hopefully though, you are choosing a different life now, and if the good values you want to bring to a relationship are truly genuine, then be courageous and declare it.

The third is the type of sex that you are having with your partner now, compared to the type of sex that you, or they, might have had with other partners. This again is a deep part of the instinct that involves competition and prowess, or maybe a sense of deficiency or inferiority. This area requires us to take great care and it might help if in a new relationship you sort of start again sexually. Don't make any comments or hints of comparison with past partners – just go into it as if its completely new for you.

The fourth issue, and probably the most common one, is simply both of you agreeing and being happy with the type and quality of sex that you are having in the relationship. If you start to have basic problems with your sexual likes and dislikes then I think you really need to ensure you are communicating about it properly and then trying earnestly to resolve things. You will perhaps have to find a middle ground for both of you, and make sure you are both happy.

All four of these issues can be difficult to discuss and damaging if left unsettled, so we must take action. With these sorts of examples in mind, start to look at your own behaviours and emotions and try as best as you can to identify anything that might be lurking in there.

Primitive Sex

Our sex drive is in essence, basic and primitive. I think that the primitive sex instinct is satisfied, and kept better in control, with primitive sex. For us in recovery, a relationship can become very deep, rich and balanced, often for the first time. We can learn things many other couples never get anywhere near understanding, particularly the true power, and joy, of the primitive sex instinct.

Occasionally in the situation of late-night pillow talk, one partner will share with the other some of their deeper sex drives, and probably feel apprehensive about expressing their thoughts. This might be a sexual fantasy that they've wanted to try out but been too shy to mention before. The first important thing to do here is remember that the question has come from the primitive part of the sex instinct and consider it from that angle rather that going straight to a surprised or disapproving response. You should respect the courage it has taken your partner to talk about a sexual fantasy. Now I'm not saying you have to do everything your partner suggests, but if your partner is not proposing anything too outrageous, but you feel apprehensive then you should ask yourself why. If you say no to most stuff then the problem is you are denying the ability of your partner, and you, to satisfy the primitive element of the instinct.

When we found sobriety, we learned that we needed a spiritual awakening to find peace. I suppose my overall proposition with this book is that the instincts of in-love, and sex, are part of that spiritual awakening. If we are partly made up of the primitive elements within those instincts, they are also part of spiritual living. If we consider how success comes about, making change and practicing the principles by replacing something that's less effective with something that's more effective, then we can see how primitive sex does fit in with these requirements. Try more basic sex, let go, be naughty and have impressive orgasms. Then see what happens to the rest of your relationship. The biggest surprise of all when you do this is an increase in your peace of mind.

Is Sex a Healing Mechanism?

What is our true opinion about the need for sex in a relationship? Our thoughts range from it being something that's largely unnecessary with no real consequence, to a real need that has to be met. Or, that it only needs to be satisfied on a physical level, or it's something that forms part of the core spiritual bond of a good relationship?

But here's the thing that I think might be the the the real added bonus with sex. What if sex between two people, properly in-love, becomes a spiritual conduit that actually has strong healing properties? Ha, I can picture the expression on your face after reading that line – it doesn't make any sense without explaining the idea. In essence the point is that if there's a problem or upset between you and your partner, try having some genuinely good and loving sex and see if that doesn't make things feel a whole lot better. To have good sex, it has to have the qualities of cherishing and respecting each other, and bring a hugely deep connection between you. So if you can make sex special like this on a good day, try repeating it when you're having a bad day. So many people withhold sex when things are going bad, like a punishment for the other person making a mistake. That's just the classic schoolboy error of two wrongs don't make a right, Love your way out of it, don't fight (remember – make love, not war).

Sometimes, if I don't have sex with my wife I feel a slight loss of connection. It's a similar feeling as the one that you get when you've had a few rough days and know you need a meeting. I feel a little troubled perhaps, and then I can feel that the sex and in-love instincts are playing on my mind. It's like an unseen resentment that I didn't know was there but now I have become aware of it. It's the same for Kathryn. For us now, the level of love and trust seems to have broken through into a higher plane – one of us can actually say, "I feel a bit disconnected, can we have sex?" And the other completely understands.

When talking to some couples though, I have found that often one person feels this disconnection feeling, and the other person is unaware or worse, isn't prepared to make it better. It can be that the men suffer this a lot more than women – it seems hard for some women to understand and accept this. When a man says he wants sex to bond and feel close, the woman doesn't always believe it, thinking he is just after the physical sex. The view taken is that men are just driven to want physical sex to sow their seed. In essence that's true - it's genetics and the drive of strong instinct. But if its denied out of hand then it's the same as denying any other instinct driven need, it pushes the instinct out of balance and that will always result in harm.

Hormones and Biological Clocks

One of the reasons we get messed up in the sex department is that we don't take a close look at the effect of hormones and our own reproductive biological clocks. And although we sometimes might talk about women's biological clocks, what about men? I recon men have biological clocks too.

Women have two biological clocks. They have the long-term fertile clock which runs from puberty to menopause and they have the monthly menstrual cycle. These cycles are driven by hormones of course, and a women's sex drive is linked to these periods of fertility by the instinctive drive to bear children. These mechanisms are important drivers to understand, and for us alcoholics, our understanding and experience is initially low. For example, some women might not feel comfortable talking to a new boyfriend about their periods. Men know the basics, but what about how it specifically effects each individual woman's libido through their monthly cycle? Do you tell your guy about that? What about when a woman reaches menopause? Things change in a woman's body but again so many women don't share these issues with their partner. Ultimately, this lack of information sharing and action falls under the category of sloth again. Women who are genuinely determined not to let these things interfere with their sex lives usually find ways to get by just fine.

But what of men's biological clocks? We've all heard of the hormone testosterone and how powerful a driver that is – any honest man will tell you that's true. This hormone drives two clocks I recon. Men have a 24-hour cycle, with peak testosterone at the end of a good nights sleep, when it's time to get up – come on girls, you know all about this one. But there also seems to be a three-day clock, and this is the important one to understand. Men seem to happily go without sex (in a good relationship) for about two days, then start to feel the want for sex by the third day. Why do I think that? Just try it out. Go four or five days between sex and I bet you the man of the relationship starts, just a little, to become restless, irritable and discontent.

Even the day after he has had sex, if he knows it will be another four days before he gets more, he will start to get tense. His security instinct tells him maybe you are rejecting him with that timescale, and he will start nagging the woman for sex. She denies him, and so you start the want-sex/no-sex merry-go-round. You see, the man thinks that other women are being inseminated by their men every three days – so he wonders what's wrong with him, why his woman doesn't want that? Can you see how perhaps the sex instinct and security instinct can be closely related in a man?

I've talked a lot throughout this book about instincts, but nothing much about hormones. We think of instincts as drivers that are one-level below our normal cognitive decision-making apparatus. So I guess that means hormones are two levels down – internal chemical drivers that we rarely discuss in recovery. But they do have emotional and mood-altering effects if you think about it. If we discount things like insulin and thyroxin, the interesting ones are testosterone, oestrogen and progesterone – and adrenalin. I'm not going to go into detail about the sex hormones, or the effects of adrenalin highs in sex, you can find out plenty on the web. I only mention them here to seed your thoughts about their functions in you and your partner.

Chapter Ten – Continuing Development

In this chapter I focus on some final key points that I think help to continue the development of relationships. Interestingly, I found at this point in the book I kept coming up with new ideas and had to make a decision to stop writing them all down. But I think we can all do this very same thing – once our recoveries and relationships get good, we will always find new ways to develop further.

Management

Let's go back to the second part of step one again. As recovering alcoholics, we are naturally weak in the department of management, so we must embrace the fact that we need to continually work at our management skills in order to sustain a good relationship. I'm talking about life management here, the sort of things that we totally neglected when we were drinking, and if we're honest, struggle with in sobriety.

Time Management

This is like a lesson in school, but it's one we need to take. We're terrible with the management of time. This defect often sits below the radar, it's not obvious at first what its effects are, plus time management clashes with the idea that we need to avoid pressures that might create panic and anxiety – we say to ourselves "it'll happen in God's time". During our drinking days we never turned up on time, never left when we should have and never paid bills by their due dates. We procrastinated, and if we started things, we never finished them. Our character defects will disrupt responsibilities that have a time element.

We often carry these faults forward into sobriety – we inventory anger and resentment until the cows come home, but planning and time-keeping, not so much. Yet deficiencies in these areas can create big problems in a relationship, so getting a grip of them is part of being responsible. General tardiness, lethargy or scatty behaviour, where we never do anything when it should be done, or when we say we're going to do it, is very destructive. It's selfish in that simple sense, where we're just constantly taking the lazy way out and not thinking about anyone else's needs at all. If we see things like this in ourselves then we must inventory accurately and then bring in the full force of step ten. I don't just mean a list at the end of the day, but a direct 'before-it-happens' action to replace the imminent time keeping failure with something that get's it done when it should get done.

Planning sensible timescales for important elements of your lives together requires discipline and effort. But we must not go overboard either – remember balance. The key is don't make it seem like a huge burden, but find ways to gently but surely achieve your aims together.

Plans and timescales are not the things to be doing in the early days but we really do need to be aware, early on, that the full force of our newly found natural instincts are going to kick in, fast – we've taken away the anaesthetic now. It's because of this that I think it's important to start outlining the issues around relationships in the early days. And then later, when it's right for us to start or rebuild a relationship, we have an idea of the link between timescales and the responsibility considerations we might be facing. Remember we've never planned anything properly before, nor thought about how long anything we were doing was going to last. So when it comes to the really big things like getting a house together, getting married or having kids, we have to get serious about the length of time such responsibilities require.

Good time management is a very hard thing for most couples to be honest about. We tend to be quite closed about our thoughts regarding when we want to do something, plan for something or to get something completed. So when one person in a relationship thinks something needs doing in a certain timescale it can be difficult to express that because they fear the other person doesn't have the same commitment to it. Very tricky, and easily the stuff of resentment.

So we can work towards more openness first, then follow that up with work on time management. Oh, and just a little observation here; have you noticed when we ask someone who's in a bit of trouble "how are you managing", what we actually mean is how are you coping, or how are you emotionally? Strangely, we never mean "how's the plan on your spreadsheet looking?"

Let's come back to the issue of the relationship itself. Just imagine two people in an early relationship with different views and feelings about it all. One might feel ready for a potential long-term commitment whereas the other might not, and feel fear about it. We say we feel trapped, or maybe we're concerned that the other person doesn't want commitment – and not know what to do about it. Then we fear that if we express those thoughts, that in itself could damage the relationship. So this is another time element that we have to be mindful of and take responsibility for. If we plan, manage and then construct this brave new world of sobriety and the possibility of a rewarding solid relationship, then we must work to remove the fear around timescales and committing to them, jointly.

198

CONTINUING DEVELOPMENT

Remember, if you can't work it out and feel excited together about it, the fear will remain. That fear will undermine the relationship, so this is the classic area where we have to replace that fear with courage. If it's done on a truly genuine basis, your higher-power will keep you safe, and deliver you to that new world.

Then comes another time question. Is it right to try and have one relationship for life, or is it right to have multiple shorter relationships? Some people argue that we are not designed to be in long-term relationships, that the desire to spread our seed is a natural one and fighting that instinct is only to consign oneself to unhappiness. Yet there are also those who believe a life-long relationship can be brilliant. But for us alcoholics, the view that it's natural to move-on is often an excuse to cover up our relationship failures. Perhaps a history of short-term relationships is similar to our tendency to do 'geographicals'. We run away from people, places and things because of fear, particularly when we mess up (only later to wallow in self-pity because we don't have what others have).

So I've come to believe that deciding what we want in terms of length of relationship is essential. In a way it's that classic romcom story where one of the characters is afraid of commitment because they're a bit of a mess, lacking in responsibility and so-on. Therefore, what must go hand-in-hand with the desire for a longer relationship is the decision to put all the work in place that is required for such a relationship. Or, put it the other way around. I think that if you don't do much work (as a recovering alcoholic), you will likely consign yourself to short relationships with lots of unhappiness. Short relationships might seem the fun choice for a while but I think either ending up in an unhappy longterm relationship, or an unhappy single life, is what happens to those that don't plan properly for a really worthwhile longterm commitment.

Managing our Finances

In many ways, financial planning goes hand-in-hand with time management. And if you get better at one, you'll likely get better at the other. We talk a lot in meetings about getting our finances back in order after our drinking days – getting a proper job to start paying the bills and rent for a new place, and then perhaps, paying off quite a lot of debt.

Paying off debt takes quite a bit of time – you might be paying things off before the start of your first proper romance. If that's the case, make sure you are honest about it right from the start, and don't risk your debt recovery plan with lots of fancy diners and holidays because that will surely backfire on you later. I have always found that honesty about something good will always get respect. Don't fear that your debt will be seen as bad, but that your debt recovery plan will be seen as good.

The business of money these days is complicated. Internet banking, credit and debit cards and payment from your smart phone (with just a little 'ting' sound). And there's shopping online, subscriptions to movie channels and downloadable apps that somehow start billing you without you really knowing why. All very convenient – at draining your money away. In early sobriety, get help with it all. Ask your sponsor or a good recovery buddy to go through it with you and eliminate anything unnecessary or wasteful. Get them to teach you how to use just the basics of modern money systems – maybe stick to one bank account with one app to manage that account online, and use only one debit card from that account. Get help to set up some simple alerts on the account that are very useful to give you warnings when you are over-spending. Then maybe go through a list of your monthly living expenses, start to budget your finances. And watch out for the temptation of credit. Credit cards, store cards and buy-now-pay-later deals are often not a wise choice for people like us. If you do need to borrow money then go very carefully and try and get a low-interest loan from your bank. Again get help from your sponsor if you need to consider a loan but also, go speak to your bank – you might be surprised how supportive they are if you explain your situation.

Now I think it goes without saying, that if you build up a good little finance management system for yourself then that's a great thing to take into a relationship. But watch out if your new found love is poor in this area. I know many people who have slowly paid off debt, and got themselves into a tidy position with their finances, only to have it all pulled down again in a new relationship. Indeed, there are many people out there who are paying off debt from past partners. So again, individual responsibility, joint responsibility, all topped-off with a frosting of even more responsibility. After picking up a drink and infidelity, the third biggest destroyer of relationships is probably financial problems. And remember, we have addictive personalities, so spending money or even gambling, will fall into that category for some of us and if that's the case it will need a full twelve step recovery programme to make progress there. Just be careful.

Interaction Processes

As we look deeper at our relationships we can examine how we interact – almost like two parts of a machine, how effective are we together. We can ask ourselves about teamwork or control, combining the best of our skills or being content together, and so-on.

Control

The topic of control needs a lot of examination for all of us in recovery – we start to learn this early in the Big Book when it talks about running the show. Stepping on other's toes is often us imparting control with our bad actions. Yet conversely, when we are told justifiably by other's that we should do something, it's often met with fierce rebellion. All part of self of course. So we start learning about letting go and becoming teachable – we soon see that doing anything at all that we haven't decided upon ourselves is a significant challenge.

This is a core element of recovery. In essence, believing that things will become better if we try to control less. We learn about the harm that control can cause, we can see illogical, power-based control as a character defect and we may have many amends to make as a result of it. We then have to find ways to practice our good principles without too much control. But we need some control, some of the time, or else we might not get important tasks done. So we're after balance, and consent. Consent is what we give when we ask someone to be our sponsor. We want that sponsor to guide us and point out our mistakes – steer us away from our defects and towards good principles. Steering is a form of control, but with responsibility and wisdom, exactly like a good captain steering a ship. It's someone else doing the serenity prayer on our behalf. Then when we sponsor, this is us having some control over someone else – it simply wouldn't work if we didn't. So in a way, this is one of the reasons why us becoming sponsors is so important – this is us practising good control, responsibility and balance – again. This brings us back to things like management and teamwork (certainly in a relationship) – two essential forms of control. But think of it more as controlling outcomes not people.

Many of us also suffer other problems from control. We might have been controlled unfairly as a child (real or imagined), faced strong sibling rivalry and bullying, or ended up in very controlling relationships. Any form of irresponsible love that contains lots of control can be hugely damaging. Maybe a partner who is extremely jealous doesn't like you meeting your friends any more, or even objects when you say hi to someone in the street, or doesn't approve of your job or, get this, even objects when you speak to others about your recovery. You must identify these sorts of problems, clearly, and either use the programme to to remove them, or ultimately if you have to, remove yourself from the problem.

Good Behaviour

We talk so much in the Fellowship about our character defects, our emotions and our spiritual wellbeing. We know we need to have a psychic change in order to successfully live the remainder of our lives with our addiction problem. We learn how we've harmed other people, and should make amends – the essence of that process being how we must become responsible for our impact on everyone else in our lives now. And of course, this is one of the main responsibilities we must carry into a relationship.

But when we go to a meeting, or meet for coffee with our sponsor, we're on our best behaviour. We are on display for these short periods of time – we switch on the good behaviour setting. Even when discussing with our sponsor our deepest character defects, and being sad or emotional about it, we're still controlling our behaviour during that short meeting.

One of my favourite rock albums is Grace Under Pressure, by the Canadian band Rush. Not everyone's cup of tea, but I love the spiritual storytelling in Rush's songs and the idea of grace under sustained long-term pressure is similar to the perfection of the prayer of St Francis – we can't attain that perfection but we should at all times keep trying. It's that sort of St Francis attitude that slowly changes our behaviour under pressure. But what pressure are we talking about in a relationship? Well, there are obvious ones like financial issues, raising kids and so-on, but also, no two people like to do the chores the same way, or watch the same stuff on TV. We have different sleep patterns and bathroom routines and when in close proximity to someone who is simply different to us, it can grate on our thoughts and feelings. When our grace is under pressure we can moan or go quiet, we can be snappy or storm off for a long walk on our own. We can be less than honest about what's wrong, or be too brutally truthful about it. We can play things down, or build them up, we can over-emphasise for dramatic effect.

If these feelings are left without some counteraction in ourselves, they will weaken our tolerance and acceptance, and then later, a worse defect may come to the surface such as anger or sulking. So behaviour is a function of our self discipline, love and acceptance, and the core of our recovery programme. It is, in essence, step ten.

Have a plan. Use the serenity prayer and the just for today card. Communicate, stay calm, think about God's love. Remember that his will for us is to carry his love and whether you really believe or not, the principle is sound - have grace as much as you can. Work together on improving both your recoveries, do service together, go out to dinner, have great sex. I suppose in a way I'm summarising what I hope to achieve with this whole book here. Maybe this book is the plan, maybe it could become part of your plan for good behaviour at least.

The results and rewards from better behaviour are truly huge. The relationship becomes positive and productive, you'll laugh a lot more, you'll feel more spiritual knowing you're really making someone else happy. That's it – your behaviour should make your partner happy, joyous and free – nothing else will do.

Bringing Out the Best in Each Other

One good test of a relationship is to see if it brings out the best in us. If you are really enjoying your time together, feeling free and loved, and giving that love back, then it brings out the best in you.

My wife and I have found this is a useful output measure on our spiritual wellbeing as a couple. We all talk about our own spiritual wellbeing, in an individual sort of way – peace of mind and conscious contact with our higher power for example. But I think spiritual wellbeing can be seen in more practical ways too. In work we might be more productive, a better team player and more creative perhaps. With our children, we might be more tolerant, more playful and more willing to teach them. In our relationship we can be more attentive, more considerate and more caring, but also very practical such as doing extra chores or surprising your partner with a gift, or dinner at a nice restaurant. Do these things and you always get something good back. It's the last part of the just for today card and it's all the quotes from the bible that say in essence "give and you shall receive".

My wife and I are aways buying each other gifts, but we do it without a sense of guilt or duty (which actually, many people do). It's much more like the three wise men bearing gifts as a celebration of love and devotion. They are good gifts – I'm not talking about a Christmas sweater that no-one really wants, but something like a good piece of jewellery that will last and be cherished. And not just at Christmas and Birthdays, indeed the best gift giving is done just because you think it's a great moment for it.

But there are times when our support can bring out the best in someone in a more serious way. Here I'm talking about actively supporting each other in situations that really matter. One classic example I think is with parenting. Parents usually don't agree with every detail about raising kids, in particular when children are a little bit naughty and then keep pushing the boundaries to perpetuate their bad behaviour. One parent usually wants to give in to that pressure whilst the other wants to "nip it in the bud" with a little more discipline. Allow this to continually happen and you will bicker, feel resentful towards each other and display all sorts of defects in front of your children – much more damaging to them than a little bit of sensible discipline when required. However, if you work constructively together to become aligned on your parenting strategy, the output of you both individually and as a team becomes much better. It quite literally brings out the best in both of you, and your kids too.

The Selfishness Paradox

There is definitely a paradoxical dimension to selfishness. We try and avoid being selfish as much as we can but if we're not careful, we end up people-pleasing too much and not expressing what we want. This can lead to a lack of clarity and frustration in a relationship. So as we build trust, we should start talking about what is selfish in a good way and what we want both for ourselves and each other. It's surprising how many people never do this and just swim around in a bog of confusion, a little bit stressed about doing the right or wrong thing and maybe starting to resent it. Work on this process early-on in your relationship, be lighthearted about it sometimes and do some things for yourself.

For example, when considering a day out, you know the sort of thing – "I don't mind where we go today, you choose." If the other person is not sure where is a good place to go, then that can be tricky for them. Agree that sometimes one of you will make a decision based on what they like, genuinely what they like, and the other will go along with it in a totally positive way. It's very refreshing to do that sometimes, and it saves on a lot of faffing.

Developing a Spiritual Relationship

Relationships are more risky than other parts of our lives because our own wellbeing is dependent on another person's spiritual and emotional condition. It's for this reason that we should develop a strong spiritual element to our relationships.

In a way, for me, finding my wife Kathryn was like finding my higher power. The higher power came first of course, in my early recovery, and that vital discovery always stands out like a beacon. The sunlight of the spirit entered my heart and gave me comfort and hope and I have a spiritual connection with my higher power whenever I need it. It's a bit like a surreal scene in a movie, when I feel pain, fear or doubt I am transported to my grassy path and my higher power is stood by my side. I briefly express my fear or ask my question and just get a knowing nod towards the right answer from him. I feel spiritually nourished and protected – it's like putting armour on.

In essence it's the same with my wife. I get a deep sense of love and understanding from her, to me. Our connection is built on the basis of us deciding we were great for each other, that we were better than the sum of the parts. That at last here was a person who took the responsibility to give me a relationship unlike anything else I had ever had before. Here was a person that was taking responsibility for my spiritual wellbeing and who regularly puts in place actions that directly improve my spiritual condition. I do the same for her. If she is unwell I mop her brow, if she needs to get anywhere I take her, if she is fearful that she has lost her way in her recovery for a moment, I help her to reconnect with her higher power. We bask together in the sunlight of the spirit.

You know absolutely if you have a spiritual bond like that with someone, or not. But what if you're in a relationship that you are rightfully rebuilding from your drinking days, but you don't feel you have the spiritual connection you would like? What can you do to try and improve that? Firstly, you have to go down that long road of increasing the other person's confidence in you. You have to drastically improve all the things that I've discussed in this book that are on your side of the street, or indeed, anywhere near your side of the street. Then you build your connection with your higher power. Build it and develop it, all the time. Make it strong, palpable and undeniable, but not overbearing or righteous. Doing God's will and administering God's love becomes your primary task. It's this process that will slowly build a spiritual bond with your partner because they will feel that change in you. Remember, when you were drinking you were the opposite of anything good or spiritual. If, in your core, you are now constantly asking your higher power for guidance and always putting other's first as in the prayer of St Francis then that will really show. Ask anyone who has genuinely done this and they will always tell you it works over time, that eventually a damaged partner will start to lose their fear of you and gain a spiritual connection with you.

The Problem with Feelings

As a basis for development, feeling are too transitory and illusory. They come from our emotions – and feed our emotions. Most relationship books seem to pivot around the idea that talking about our feelings somehow solves problems but this process, in isolation, doesn't work –

when I hear other people discussing their relationship problems based on feelings, it just seems to lead to confusion, conflict and fear.

In early recovery we start to pull back on our worst defects, our core selfishness and unmanageability. But when we get properly to step four and five, and work on that area for the first time, we start to see the real mechanics of our personality. Prior to this, we really have no idea where our feelings are coming from and for the first time, start to recognise that the feelings are the symptoms not the cause. Once we have our inventory in some detail we can start steps six and seven – replacing our clearly identified defects with something better.

For me, this is when I started to see that feelings based on those bad inventory items are just a liability. The truth is there are often a pair of defects together – the real defect itself, and the incorrect feeling that goes with it. As I have slowly replaced bad stock with good, my feelings have changed too. Indeed the mechanism of having feelings is different. I understand now that feelings should be based on reasonably well-balanced instincts, and a peaceful spiritual condition. They are different feelings now, not so wildly emotional or up-and-down, and certainly not fearful. They come from contentment and a gentle flow of happiness.

How often have you found that as a relationship gets going, your feelings start to spiral out of control? Sure, you might be feeling things such as love and attraction at the beginning but after a while the closeness can start to get more difficult to deal with – not easier. Our sensitivities to things like criticism, having to compromise and worries about sex will rapidly trigger feelings. And whilst I'm not suggesting we take no account of those feelings, we must make sure we work backwards from them to find the underlying causes.

STEVE E

Fear and Freedom

One evening, after a meeting when we were clearing up the chairs and coffee cups, the topic of relationships was the discussion. A few people had shared about problems in their relationships during the meeting. I made a simple statement to which the result was profound. I said "the core issue with relationships seems to be fear". They all agreed strongly, in unison and with some surprise, it was literally a collective lightbulb moment.

This fear is, I think, similar to the fear we have in early recovery when we consider the wreckage of our past. There seems to be too much damage and so, too much guilt remembering what we did. Then the task to re-design our personality seems monumental; almost impossible even though we can see the astonishing results in our fellows around us. It's the same feeling that we have when we consider relationships. Relationships seem baffling, driven by emotion and desire and appear risky for building up dependancies and commitments. That perceived burden creates fear. But then we also have the fear of loneliness and lack of fulfilment if we don't have a relationship.

One of the biggest ways to counteract fear in a relationship might be to generate good and appropriate levels of freedom between you. Of course I don't mean freedoms that are wrong and would cause hurt (like infidelity), I mean freedoms with responsibility. If you have good responsibility then you should be able to have high levels of freedom. For a start, what you say about yourself to your partner should be similar to what you say to your sponsor. You have to honestly share what you are, admit your faults, discuss how you are working on them, and ask for forgiveness when you make mistakes. And equally your partner should be that open with you. Your acceptance of each other, for what you are, and

210

the complete openness about it all, is the core of your freedom. A lack of freedom is quite literally being trapped, like in a dungeon, so don't create the trap. Let your partner know that you will do your best to protect what's right for them and if necessary, not stand in the way of any future decisions they might have to make.

And They Lived Happily Ever After

There are fairytales. All of us in recovery do, in a sense, live a fairytale. Through years and years of torment at the hands of our demons, we are chased to the gates of doom. Then, by some miracle, we find a way to escape. First we run and hide, still trembling with fear, but later we find kindly friends and start a journey together. They take us to pastures new and teach us how to keep safe, how to nurture and how to build. We pull together and discover a new life with each other. And we find ourselves.

Okay, enough, or I'll be writing a screenplay next. But look, the point of a fairytale is that we always go off into the sunset with the love of our life. So we'd better take a look at how we might live happily ever after. Fundamentally I think a relationship has to transition from being a big deal, a commitment and an effort, into becoming our normal living. The work at the start is the bridge, all this book is the bridge, but we must make sure we arrive. We will never be at peace if we don't.

So developing the relationship at depth should have its sights on the end-game. But what might that look like? Let me start with what my day is like. I wake in a lovely bedroom, it's ornate features and restful colours in our 19th century Georgian house are soothing, but also a direct reminder of my own efforts to create it – I renovated all the fittings and decorated the room myself. My wife awakes as the cat jumps up on our bed. We usually rise rather spritely, one of us showering first whilst the other gets the espresso underway. We get good summers here on the Isle of Wight, so we often drink our first coffee out in the garden, in the early-morning sun. Kathryn feeds the fish. We've usually got a rough idea of what we want to do with our day, and that might be visiting friends or family, me doing some writing or other office work, or us both doing something together out, like long county walks or a shopping trip to one of the big cities on the mainland (with an enjoyable little boat-trip either way).

Kathryn works part-time, mainly because she enjoys the work, and I guess you would say I am semi-retired. We are very lucky in that we are financially secure (now). So our days are flexible and safe, fun and gentle, with no big panics or fearful things occurring. We often talk in the solution of recovery – that is, we mention a little the improvements we have made in our peace-of-mind or something about our daily readings. And we enjoy stuff, the garden, going to church, or a meeting. A good home-cooked meal and a funny movie ends the day. But also life is incredibly exciting on a bigger scale. We're creative. Kathryn is studying law and criminology and I write books and develop businesses. We both work in the development of recovery thinking, and occasionally that takes us on trips far and wide.

But of course, we're still alcoholics. So at times we are childish, grandiose or over-sensitive. Maybe that has to be there, else we might forget what we really are. So when our behaviour slips a little, we usually deal with it by reminding ourselves of two things – to be responsible and that it will pass.

The being responsible bit means to us now, to do our duty. Keeping 'our side of the street clean' has taken on a clearer, shorter sort of character. We don't need to analyse too much what we need to do, we've been there before, we know what to do. Like a soldier, we fall back on our training because the training is what brings the result.

CONTINUING DEVELOPMENT

Letting things pass works so well because it suggest that the problem, what ever it is, is in motion. It's not going to hang around. Not one of the myriad of problems we used to have are around now, so why should the next one be any different? This is probably the biggest point of all with the living happily ever after thing. Our bridge to normal living tasks, including developing a relationship, should in the end, get us to the far side of all our big problems, and then, as the small ones come along, we just waive them by.

Chapter Eleven – Conclusion

Looking back now I can see that the primary purpose of writing this book was for my own development with relationships. I'd made an awful mess of relationships before I found recovery and wanted to do so much better in sobriety.

At the beginning I worked the steps, found a higher-power and carried the message. But then it turned out that what was most important of all was finding 'the wisdom to know the difference'. Just like with every other aspect of life, I'd learned nothing of any use during my youth and through my drinking days about relationships. So I researched, analysed, mapped-out connections and started to built a process that made sense. And then I felt a calling, driven by my higher power, to write it all down.

I started the book by trying to capture all the relevant introductory points. The basics of why we want relationships. I also realised that practical situations vary greatly with our relationships in early recovery, so I suggested the idea that we must start by assessing our situations with real honesty. And we need a clear idea of the responsibility that relationships require for ourselves and our partners.

Then of course there was another major element at play with relationships – and that was instincts. We talk about instincts at a basic level in recovery, but I felt we needed a lot more understanding in this area. I also came to believe that this analysis is a much more effective if we add a fourth instinct – the 'in-love' instinct. By doing this I found I could reconcile far more effectively our drives and behaviours. I also found it incredibly important to understand the differences between men and women – how we think differently. We have to learn not to judge 'man-brain' and 'woman-brain' behaviour, but to embrace it.

Then I found that because partnerships are such a significant challenge, we need to bring extra clarity and focus when working our recovery in relationships. In a relationship our lives are far more complex and we are much more exposed to someone else's character defects. Equally, it's much easier for our own untreated defects to have a negative impact on a partner. I realised that to achieve effective action and results together we need to actually do the steps together, or at least what I call 'the steps overlay', where you add elements to the steps that help with the development of joint security and wellbeing.

Next I expanded on the idea of defects and their opposite principles. Here I found that there was no point in my writing in general terms, so I described all of the defects and principles I have developed for myself, with specific elements in each of them for relationships.

I then went on to discuss more ideas about self. Our self-will and and self-centred traits – good and bad. I found that when we analyse 'self' based on things like selfishness or self-sacrifice we gain another dimension on how we function as humans, and how we might become better prospects for a relationship.

Then in the book I changed tack. I came on to practical matters in a way that focusses on getting real situations changed for the better. Often in recovery we don't do this very well – and although this doesn't matter so much if we are single, it can have a big negative effect if relationships don't take practical change forward.

Then I talk about sex. I found in my research that we don't talk about the problems of sex as an instinct, and a conflicting driver of desire and fear, anywhere near enough. It takes a bit of effort and genuine soul-searching to make progress on the sex front, but just think how many couples suffer terribly with sex problems that almost inevitably lead to failure in the relationship. If we're not prepared to suffer failure at the hands of alcohol, why should we have any less resolve against our problems with sex?

Then in the last chapter I discuss some further points that I think help with the deeper development of relationships, and hopefully show how any of us can then keep improving the structure and happiness of the lives that we share with someone else.

But now it's time to draw to a close:

Many people have asked me why I wrote this book – "Steve, why did you go to so much effort and what do you hope it will it achieve?"

Well, the first two problems for anyone who gets a calling to do something, is that it's always an awful lot of work and you can't seem to let yourself out of it. It's like the folks who do AA projects for public information, work in prisons or plan annual conventions say, you could ask them why they are so driven to do those difficult tasks. I think its partly carrying the message and giving away what we so gratefully received, but you can do that to great effect by sharing in meetings every week. My church friends say that when you are called to action by God, it's inspirational, creative, the proper use of your skills, but also non-negotiable – it's what Bill W said happened to him. But the other main element, perhaps the biggest one, is its a huge bridge to normal living – it is in fact, living the dream. As you get into this sort of thing you meet incredible new people, you find out new things you never knew before, all the time. It's invigorating, you get fired-up, your life gets exciting and you look back on your past and you can see more and more clearly what it was all for.

CONCLUSION

At first I didn't really know why I thought the problem of relationships was so important. I just did. My relationship experiences took me down that path to start with and then as I worked, I could see a better way forward for me, and maybe other alcoholics too. There seemed to be a vast shortfall in our understanding and willingness to work properly with relationships.

So what do I hope this book will achieve? I hope it shares, between me and you, some new ideas. Maybe it will shed some clear light on worries about relationships for you. It might give you strength to make some important changes that you need to make. It might help you work with other recovering alcoholics who are struggling with relationships. But more than that I hope it forms part of your bridge to normal living and enables you to achieve more of the promises – with someone you love.

And just maybe the book will help all the people around you, and the people in the future whom you haven't met yet. Maybe a new wife or husband and a big new family who are simply going to experience something wonderful as you come into their lives. Love and peace – lives beyond their wildest dreams too.

STEVE E

References

Alcoholics Anonymous, third edition, New York, Alcoholics Anonymous World Services, Inc, 1976. (The Big Book)

Twelve Steps and Twelve Traditions, New York, Alcoholics Anonymous World Services, Inc, 1981. (The Twelve and Twelve)

The Best of Bill, New York, The AA Grapevine Inc, 1990.

Carry This Message, Joe McQ, Atlanta, August House Publishers, 2002.

Drop The Rock, Bill P, Todd W, Sara S, second edition, Hazelden Publishing, 2005.

Why Men Don't Listen & Women Can't Read Maps, Allan and Barbara Pease, publisher Orion, 2017.

Men Are from Mars, Women Are from Venus, John Gray, publisher HarperCollins, 1992.

Big Book Study Tapes, Joe and Charlie, various IOS and Android apps.

Printed in Great Britain
by Amazon